A Philosophy
   of ADULT
      CHRISTIAN
      EDUCATION

A Philosophy
of ADULT
CHRISTIAN
EDUCATION

by

David J. Ernsberger

Philadelphia

THE WESTMINSTER PRESS

© W. L. JENKINS MCMLIX

Scripture quotations from the Revised Standard Version of the Bible are copyright, 1946 and 1952, by the Division of Christian Education of the National Council of Churches, and are used by permission.

LIBRARY OF CONGRESS CATALOG CARD NO. 59–9090

PRINTED IN THE UNITED STATES OF AMERICA

In grateful memory of
LEWIS JOSEPH SHERRILL
1893–1957
Adviser, Inspirer, and Friend

Contents:

Preface:

THIS book grew out of an extended research program undertaken at Union Theological Seminary in New York City. I worked on the project off and on for two years while serving as assistant pastor at the Bryn Mawr Park Presbyterian Church in Yonkers, New York. It represented the insights resulting from a combination of research in the field of adult education and experience as minister of education in a local church.

With the encouragement of Rev. William C. Schram, Secretary of the Department of Adult Program of the Board of Christian Education of The United Presbyterian Church U.S.A., and Dr. Roland W. Tapp, Associate Religious Book Editor, The Westminster Press, I have simplified and developed it to its present form. It now reflects further research in the field, and further experience as an adult educator in a new church I have recently organized in Saginaw, Michigan. My people here in Countryside Church have not been aware of it, but they have been most helpful in the testing of some of the ideas advanced in this book. A new church, free for the stereotyped forms of program and organization that so often stand in the way of significant adult education work in older churches, provides a wonderful opportunity for experimentation with new forms and contents.

This is emphatically not another how-to-do-it book, in the ordinary sense of the term. It is a book in the field of practical theology in that it attempts that difficult but eminently necessary feat of being at once theological and practical. It seeks to relate some key theological, sociological, and psychological insights (including some group dynamics theories) to an understanding of our task as adult educators in the local church. That sounds like a large order, I know. And it would be, if every aspect were treated exhaustively (and exhaustingly). However, I have written this only to start others along a line of thinking that each will develop differently in practice, but that has been immensely influential in shaping my own conception of my total ministry. This book does not have all the answers; but I believe it raises some of the most important questions concerning our teaching ministry. If it serves as a stimulus to thought and action, to further experimentation and discovery, writing it will have been worth-while.

DAVID J. ERNSBERGER

Saginaw, Michigan

Introduction:

ONE of the most significant yet generally overlooked aspects of the Protestant Reformation in the sixteenth century was the renewed emphasis on general adult religious education which attended it. During the Middle Ages, monasteries and great universities had emerged as centers of learning; but on the local parish level, adult learning had decreased almost to the vanishing point. The Protestant Reformation spelled a reversal of this trend and a recovery of the emphasis on adult instruction that had characterized the first centuries of the Christian Era. In the churches of the Reformation, an informed laity, well-versed in the Bible and in the confessions and catechisms based on it, was held to be as essential as an informed ministry.

Adult instruction continued to receive great emphasis well into the post-Reformation period, but by the middle of the nineteenth century it had generally declined in importance as an aspect of church life. The growth of the adult Sunday school movement in the latter half of the nineteenth century helped to counteract this trend to some extent. But in terms of numbers involved and breadth and variety of program, the adult education movement as we know it is actually a fairly recent development in Protestantism, even though it may be regarded as being, in many ways, a return to some of the emphasis of the earlier years of the post-Reformation period.

Only within the past three decades has the concept of adult Christian education generally come to have a more inclusive meaning than simply a reference to the traditional Sunday morning adult Bible class. Early in the 1930's a few pioneers in the field began to point out the inadequacies of the stereotyped adult Bible class as the sole medium of adult Christian education. These educators felt that the traditional adult Bible class, which so often consisted mainly of a lecture followed by a few perfunctory questions and answers, was not meeting the deeper religious needs of adults. They banded together to form the United Christian Adult Movement in 1938, and this organization played an important part in broadening the scope of adult Christian education to include such areas of concern as family-life education, social education and action, the training of church officers and teachers, and adult church membership classes.

As local churches increasingly expanded their programs of adult education into these areas, denominational and interdenominational boards were called upon to produce an ever-growing flood of resource and study materials. In addition, the curriculums for adult Bible classes began to undergo significant changes. As the uniform lesson approach became more and more discredited in educational circles, the editors of adult curriculum materials followed the lead of the editors of the children's materials and began to experiment with other types and arrangements of content. Beginning in 1948, for example, the Presbyterian *Christian Faith and Life* curriculum for adults provided a topical, thematic approach to Biblical content to satisfy those who had begun to realize the limitations of the uniform lesson materials. This made possible a more systematic approach to Biblical theology than could be achieved with the uniform lesson arrangement of Biblical content. Provision was made for the special needs and interests of young adult groups by including a separate course of study for them. The new Seabury curriculum of the Protestant Episcopal Church has sought a closer and more meaningful correlation of the curriculum of adult classes with that of the children's departments than had been achieved through the correlated three-year cycle of the *Christian Faith and Life* curriculum for children and adults and its magazines for parents. However, in 1957, the *Christian Faith and Life* curriculum magazine for adults was expanded to include resource materials for parents' discussion groups, relating Christian doctrine to typical situations and problems in family life. In both denominations, the curriculum editors are in the vanguard of those who are trying to think through and apply a systematic and relevant philosophy of adult education.

But the ever-increasing flood of materials published by the denominations has not solved the problems of the local church in the area of adult education. These materials have generally been produced in response to a widespread but unstructured demand from the churches; and with the exception of the two denominations noted above, the philosophy behind them seems to be as formless as the demand that called them into being. But the confusion of purpose behind the profusion of materials is as nothing compared to the absence of a coherent philosophy of adult education which seems to typify the average minister and his parish program. One indication of the way in which the local church tends to lag behind the denominational curriculum planners is to be seen in the fact that uniform lesson materials continue to be the mainstay of study in adult church school classes, even though the denominations are increasingly offering curricular alternatives that are more relevant to basic adult needs. Earl F. Zeigler recently polled a number of denominational adult curriculum editors, who reported that 100 per cent, 95 per cent, 85 per cent, 75 per cent, and, in a few cases, 50 per cent of their adult church school classes were still using uniform lesson materials.[1]

A few significant books have been written in recent years which are helpful for pastors who are seeking to formulate a philosophy of Christian education *in general* which will reflect the fresh insights of the contemporary theological revival. However, hardly anything of great significance has been written by Christian educators in recent years dealing with the *specific* and somewhat *unique* problems of formulating a philosophy of *adult* Christian education that reflects some of this new theological light. Much that is valid for the Christian education of children in such important recent works as James D. Smart's *The Teaching Ministry of the Church* and Lewis J. Sherrill's *The Gift of Power* is equally valid for a philosophy of Christian adult education; yet their basic insights need to be developed further in relation to the specific area of adult work, and supplemented by other relevant material.

The purpose of this book is to set forth a tentative working philosophy of adult education for the local church. Such a philosophy, it seems to me, should be based on (1) a clarification of the doctrine of the church and its ministry as this bears upon the church's educational responsibility to its adults; (2) an analytical understanding of our laymen's basic needs; and (3) an examination of the unique contributions that small groups in the church can make in accomplishing the church's task of relating the content of the Christian faith to these needs.

First of all, since the quality and nature of the adult program will depend in large measure upon what the minister does about it, his self-image and his doctrine of the ministry and of the church play an important part in a philosophy of adult education. We are all well aware that there is considerable variation both within and among denominations on these matters. However, recent ecumenical conferences in this country and abroad have indicated that there is a surprisingly large area of essential agreement among the major Protestant communions concerning doctrines of the church and its ministry. Now, of course, a least-common-denominator approach to denominational mergers is rightly discredited by those who take theological concerns seriously. However, such an approach has considerable validity as a means for developing a philosophy of Christian education, the relevance of which will not be confined along denominational lines. Therefore the doctrines of the church and its ministry that are related to the task of adult Christian education in this book are those generally held in common by the major denominational families of Protestant Christianity. The doctrinal differences that do exist concerning these matters are very real and important, but they have little bearing on a philosophy of adult Christian education.

Secondly, in addition to doctrines of the church and its ministry, an adequate philosophy of adult Christian education must also be based upon an understanding of the problems and needs of the adult layman at various levels. Such a philosophy must, at least, reflect an awareness of contemporary sociological, economic, and cultural influences upon him. It must also take into consideration the conscious interests of adults and the expectations these laymen tend to have in relation to their church and their minister. Generalizations, of course, are always somewhat precarious. There is a certain degree of variation among all these factors because of differences in age, socioeconomic status, and the type of community in which each particular church is located. But since white-collar and gray-collar urban and suburban communities constitute the living and working environment of the great majority of our adults, the analysis of their current problems and needs will be centered there. However, our understanding of the adult layman would be ephemeral and superficial indeed if it did not also include an analysis of the more *enduring* psychological and spiritual predicaments of modern man, whether he be white-collar or gray-collar, suburban or rural. Part of the soul-sickness of our adults is confined to urban and suburban life in mid-twentieth-century America. Another part of it is confined to the centuries since the Renaissance. Still another part of it is as old as human life itself. We must understand the needs and problems of the adult at every level of his existence.

Finally, after we have attained a clearer view of the church and its ministry, and of the adults we would serve, we will be in a position to explore the many ways in which the church and its ministry can mediate God's redemption and reconciliation to laymen through the program of Christian education. In this regard, special attention will be given to the functioning and the potentialities of small study groups in the church, and in conclusion some general observations will be made concerning further implications of this philosophy for parish organization and program.

CHAPTER ONE:

The Role of the Minister in the Local Church

SAMUEL BLIZZARD'S study of a large sample group of seminary graduates indicates a widespread perplexity and vagueness among ministers today concerning the roles they are to perform. There has been a great proliferation of new roles thrust upon the minister during the past fifty years. As Blizzard points out, the traditional office of the ministry consisted essentially of just three roles: the minister as preacher, as priest (i.e., as leader in public worship), and as teacher.[2] The past half century has witnessed the gradual emergence of several new roles which the minister is expected to perform. In addition to the traditional roles, the average minister is now increasingly expected to function as organizer of an ever-growing number of parish activities, as administrator of the consequently more complex church, and as a counselor in personal problems. In response to these newly emphasized role expectations which arose among the laymen of the churches, and, to a lesser degree, among the ministers themselves, theological seminaries during the past two generations have added a multitude of new courses to their curriculum offerings. One can now find many courses in Christian education, parish organization and administration, and pastoral counseling in the catalogues of seminaries that offered very few of these fifty years ago. The seminaries have generally responded to these new demands simply by adding new courses to the curriculum, without seeking to relate them theologically to the older and more traditional disciplines.[3] In the same manner, the parish minister has tended to respond passively by merely adding these new and time-consuming role emphases to the older roles without integrating them theologically into a self-conscious and systematic doctrine of the ministry.

It is imperative that all these ministerial roles be arranged into a hierarchy of values, a scale of priorities. Otherwise, the only alternatives are either to give exactly the same amount of time to each of these roles (which would imply that each is of exactly the same value) or else to have the amount of time spent on each determined by the relative strength of all the external pressures and demands upon his time that the minister faces daily.

Indeed, Blizzard's study seems to indicate that the latter alternative is very frequently chosen. Instead of being the *initiators of change* in the relative time distribution made between the various ministerial roles, the ministers in his survey tended to respond quite passively to the role expectations of their parishioners and their communities, and the program pressures exerted by their denominational boards.[4] Referring to some of the respondents in Blizzard's survey, H. Richard Niebuhr states that those who refuse to conform passively to the role expectations of lay groups in their churches and the subtle pressures of denominational program promotion and of the wider community often say they have had to do this entirely by themselves. They have had to work out their own standards as to which aspects of their work deserve more time and which deserve less, without any real help from their seminary training. They declare that the maintenance of their sense of specific vocation is a highly personal responsibility. They believe that the overbusyness of many of their ministerial colleagues and the great sense of pressure under which these men work may be caused by their failure to develop any firm principles of judgment for parceling out their working time among the functions they are expected to perform.[5]

In every aspect of his work, the minister needs to face the problem of determining who he is and what he is primarily trying to achieve. He needs some transcendent standard of judgment for distinguishing the more important from the less important within the complexity of his functions. But in practice, Blizzard's survey indicates that the minister generally has no such central focus around which to integrate and arrange his activities. This does *not* mean that the minister has no personal scale of values, no *preferences* among the many roles he is called upon to perform. For example, the survey indicates that ministers greatly prefer preaching to administrative work, and regard it as much more important. But although the minister has a definite scale of personal preferences and values, he has no clearly defined *functional priorities* to which he adheres despite the many social pressures exerted upon him. This is clearly indicated by the notable disparity between the relative importance of the various ministerial roles in the minister's own scale of preferences and the relative proportions of his time actually devoted to each.

According to Blizzard's survey, the average minister regards the preaching role as being of first importance, followed in order by the roles of pastor, priest, organizer, administrator, and finally teacher. But the time the average minister in the survey actually spends in performing these roles is distributed in a quite different order. The order from most time-consuming to least time-consuming is as follows: administrator, pastor, preacher and priest, organ-

izer, and teacher.[6] The minister thus divides his time among
his various roles, not in accordance with his personal scale
of values and preferences, but in accordance with the demands that others make upon his time. Blizzard's study also
indicates an almost perfect correlation between the relative
ordering of roles according to the *importance* ascribed to
them and the relative ordering of the roles according to the
satisfaction derived from them.

It is particularly noteworthy that the *teaching role* of
the ministry *received less average time than any of the
other five major ministerial roles considered in this study*,
and that it was regarded by the respondents as being *the
least important and least satisfying* of their duties. This
tendency to minimize the teaching role of the ministry has,
as we shall see, unfortunate effects upon the minister's
functioning in his other roles.

Another significant indication to be derived from Blizzard's survey is the fact that next to the teaching role, the
role of the minister as organizer receives the least amount
of his time. As organizer, the minister works with small
groups of officers and program planners in directing the
organizational life of the church. Of all his major roles,
only the organizational and teaching roles involve the minister in work with *small primary groups* in the church.
The work of the minister as administrator, pastor-counselor, preacher, and leader in public worship does not consist in working with small face-to-face groups. Blizzard
defines the administrative role, as distinct from the organizational role, as including all those functions which do not
involve direct contact with parishioners, and as we have
seen, this role is the most time-consuming according to the
survey. As pastor-counselor, the minister works with individuals. As preacher and leader in worship, he ministers to
the entire congregation. Therefore the fact that the roles

of organizer and teacher are regarded as least significant and satisfying, and receive the least amount of the minister's time, indicates that *the primary or face-to-face group life of the church is minimized in favor of the ministry to individuals on the one hand and to the entire congregation on the other.*

Thus a relative vacuum exists between the congregation and the individual. Ministers tend to neglect the importance of the small groups which can serve to mediate between the congregation as a whole and the individual member. This minimizing of the small-group life of the church is particularly lamentable since it is within small groups that the minister may best function in the role of adult educator.

The prevalent tendency to regard as least important those roles which involve the minister in work with intimate primary groups has a number of other unfortunate consequences for the life of the church. One of these consequences is the highly individualistic attitude so often taken toward the role of pastor-counselor. The minister tends to view both himself and his counselee as isolated individuals rather than in terms of more inclusive social relationships within the church. He sees his counseling ministry as a function directed wholly toward individuals, rather than toward small groups of individuals. Wayne E. Oates, in his book *Anxiety in Christian Experience,* maintains that ministers often fail to see the church itself, in its entirety and especially in its primary group life, as a potentially therapeutic community which should be vitally concerned with the quality of all its interpersonal relationships. They seem to be unaware that their counseling work is essentially a function of the entire church as a Christian fellowship and not simply that of the pastor as an isolated individual. Because they do not adequately realize the therapeutic potential inherent in small groups within the church, which could supplement their own efforts to help people, they feel they must carry the entire counseling load on their own shoulders. And because they do not regard their counseling ministry as a function that also involves their relationship with small groups of individuals within the church, they are likely to neglect the less clamorous needs of a greater number of persons while they minister to a few counselees who have come to them individually.[7]

Such an individualistic conception of the counseling role is probably caused by the fact that in the mind of the minister it is dissociated from his other more communal roles. The minister who has no coherent picture of the interrelatedness of his various roles will not be likely to see the relationship between his role as educator and his role as physician of the soul. He will be oblivious to the potentially therapeutic and preventive value of educational processes in small groups, as the shared life of such groups ministers to psychological needs. Oates warns that certain failures of communication may occur between minister and counselee when the minister deals with individuals as though he were not the representative of the congregation, and if he has not developed a program of adult education that indirectly supplements his counseling work.

> For instance, certain premarital counseling procedures with individuals can very easily create such misunderstandings if the pastor has not developed a church-wide program of family life education along with his private counseling. If he has done this, then the corporate life of the church is more likely to be edified . . . and to accept and understand what he is striving to do for them.[8]

Furthermore, whenever a minister is counseling disturbed people whose problems are within the realm of his competence, the right kind of group experience in the church can buttress his efforts in aiding them along the road to recovery. According to Oates, a majority of the persons whose spiritual encounters with anxiety he has witnessed as a counselor have expressed a need to become a part of an intimate fellowship of Christians who have had similar experiences.

It is quite likely that the counseling load of many ministers could be lightened if they were to discover that small study groups can be very useful in supplementing the processes of individual guidance and counseling. A group of people who are seeking Christian answers to the same general sort of problem may be of inestimable help to one another in attaining creative new adjustments. In the profound sharing of personal experience and insights that is possible in such a group, members have an excellent opportunity to observe the Biblical injunction to " Bear one another's burdens, and so fulfil the law of Christ " (Gal. 6:2).

But because there is a gap between the minister's image of himself as counselor and as educator, there is likewise a tragic gap between the aching loneliness of many anxious individuals and some of the potential corporate resources of the Christian fellowship. Often these people earnestly desire to communicate with others about the central issues of life, even though they may not be completely conscious of having this desire. But in any case, they are often too concerned about themselves and what other people think of them to make the enormous effort required to establish meaningful personal relationships within the maze of superficial contacts that often passes for " fellowship " in the church. They move on, lonely in the midst of many people and organizations, and anxious about something, they know not what. When their craving for fellowship and supportive friendships is satisfied more through participation in secular groups than in church groups, it is time for the church to examine itself critically. Many people are finding in nonchurch groups the kind of acceptance and intimate Christian warmth they hear defined, but seldom implemented, in the church.

Small groups are essential links between the individual layman and the impersonal, complicated institutional and social structure of the church. More will be said in another chapter concerning the therapeutic implications of adult Christian education in small groups. But the point is sufficiently clear that to play down both the minister's role as educator and the intimate group life of the church weakens the effectiveness of the minister in his role as pastor-counselor, and perhaps needlessly increases the amount of time he must spend in the performance of this role.

A second unfortunate consequence of this tendency to minimize the importance of primary groups in the life of the church is the failure of the church to minister adequately to the family as an integral social unit. This is especially unfortunate since the family is doubtless the most important and formative primary group in the church. In New Testament times, people frequently entered the church as members of households rather than as individuals. In the book of The Acts, the accounts of the entire households of Cornelius, Lydia, and the Philippian jailer following them in their commitment to Christ and his church are but three instances of this tendency. And until comparatively recently in Christian history, the teaching ministry of the church was directed primarily toward households rather than toward individuals. Yet in the present day, the individualistic mind-set of the minister often results in the organization of parish life in such a way that the family unit is atomized and torn asunder nearly every night of the week, and twice on Sundays. The quite laudable return to family worship services and the current emphasis on church family night programs in many churches has only partially counteracted this tendency.

In the area of Christian education, the minister in his role as educator has tended to bypass the family unit as a whole in an effort to educate the child as an isolated individual, apart from the family group. The idea of the " child-centered church," championed by George Albert Coe and his disciples, has enjoyed quite a vogue in the past two generations. But in 1940, H. Shelton Smith launched an epoch-making criticism against this point of view. He maintained that periods of great religious rebirth have not emerged in the history of the church as a result of child nurture, but through a religious transformation of adults that usually involved a break with the religion that they themselves had inherited from their own childhood. " This means," he said, " that unless the faith comes alive in the soul of some mature individual or group, religious vitality may be expected to decline in modern culture. . . . For the religion of the child will usually be a relatively pale edition of the faith of the older generation." [9]

Increasingly, religious educators are coming to see that the idea of the " child-centered " church must be supplanted by the idea of the " family-centered " church, since the program of Christian education for children will be quite limited in its effectiveness without a parallel program of parent education. A spur to this gradual change in emphasis has come through the impact in Christian education circles of Reuel Howe's book *Man's Need and God's Action*. The central thesis of this book is that Christian education does not take place in a social vacuum but in the midst of a life of personal, primary group relationships which condition the process either positively or negatively. The nature of the relationships between adults and children in the home — whether they are characterized by love or hostility, trust or fear, etc. — largely conditions and determines what is actually communicated through the words and other symbols of the faith that parents and church school teachers use. For this reason, the minister in his teaching role should be as much concerned about the quality of the personal interrelationships in the home as he should be about the religious literacy of the parents, who are, at least, potentially the chief communicators of the faith. Indeed, the two cannot be separated in parents' groups without falling either into a this-is-how-to-raise-your-children moralism or into theological speculation that has no obvious relevance to the problems of these relationships in the home. Discussions should relate Christian beliefs meaningfully and organically to developmental psychology and other disciplines that shed light on family life problems.

Judging from the picture of the average pastor which emerges from Blizzard's study, we see that religious educators who are writing in this field of family life education seem to be far ahead of him in their appreciation of the importance of the ministry to the family as a whole and in its corollary of a renewed emphasis on adult education. Back in 1946, Wesner Fallaw declared in *The Modern Parent and the Teaching Church* that the crucial problem of Christian education lies in educating the whole family, not just the individual child. Family-centered Christian education requires a strong program of adult education, with the education of children its by-product, so to speak. Fallaw believes that the education of adults in small parents' groups should receive even more attention and emphasis in the parish program than the church school itself.[10] Many other educators would agree with him, at least to the extent of saying that the adult education program of the churches needs to be much more strongly emphasized, and that the most effective way for the minister to discharge his educational responsibility toward the children of his parish is through the Christian education of their parents and church school teachers.

Lewis J. Sherrill maintains that the teaching ministry must begin with adults for the simple reason that as parents they are the child's first teachers, and because the nature of the system of personal interaction in the home will greatly influence what the child appropriates from the more formal teaching of the church school.[11] Frank W. Herriott, his colleague at Union Seminary, likewise has said that churches would do well to alter the goals of their total educational programs away from such a dominant emphasis on the education of children and toward giving a much higher priority to the Christian education of the adult congregation. However, the unfortunate fact is that in the average church, adult education is given a low priority in terms of estimated importance and in terms of the proportion of the minister's time devoted to it. Very often it receives an even smaller proportion of his time than the Christian education of the children in the church.

A third consequence of the tendency to neglect work with primary groups is a lack of co-ordination and purpose in the programs of the various voluntary adult organizations in the parish. We noted earlier that the ministers in Blizzard's survey rated the organizational role of the minister very low in importance, and that this role stood next to the bottom in the amount of time actually spent on it. This lack of emphasis on the role of the minister as organizer frequently finds expression in a laissez-faire, " hands-off " attitude toward the program-planning of the various adult organizations. It is not surprising, therefore, that program committees, lacking the advice and assistance of the minister, often plan programs that are wholly secular and quite unrelated to the central purposes for which the church exists. How often in the churches we see couples clubs whose programs are purely social and recreational; men's clubs whose monthly supper meetings are almost indistinguishable in program content from meetings of some secular service club; women's groups which, after opening with a brief " devotional," as it is often called, spend the rest of their time planning and working on money-raising projects!

It is very convenient to blame the secular nature of many of the programs in the voluntary adult organizations in the churches upon the supposedly secular presuppositions of the lay people who plan them. Yet it might be closer to the truth to suggest that they very often choose such programs by default because the minister has not suggested to them alternative program resources that are more religiously significant in content.

The program-planning of the various church organizations offers an excellent opportunity for adult Christian education, an opportunity not only for educating the general membership of these organizations through the selection of religiously meaningful programs, but also, and especially, for educating the program planners themselves in responsible and informed churchmanship. In other words, it affords the minister an opportunity for educating the " educators " of the great majority of the adults in his church, since these program planners determine the content and quality of most of the learning opportunities that the church offers its adults. This is not meant to imply that the minister should dictate the content of organizational programs in an authoritarian manner; but surely he should make himself readily available as a resource person in a democratic process of program-planning within the context of the small, official groups normally responsible for such planning. The minister should actively encourage all program planners to avail themselves of the program ideas he is uniquely capable of giving. However, the average minister will " simply not have time enough " for this work if he continues to minimize the importance of his role as organizer.

We have taken a look at the problem of role priorities as it affects the ministry today. We have noted that the minister faces a conflict in the actual apportionment of his working hours: a conflict between his *idealized* image of himself as primarily a preacher and pastor-counselor, and his *functional* estimate of himself as primarily an administrator " just keeping the parish wheels turning." The minister has tended to accommodate his own role preferences rather passively to the role expectations imposed on him by others. The roles of the minister as organizer and as educator have received relatively little emphasis from either clergy or laymen, and this has resulted in a tendency to minimize the work of the minister with small groups within the framework of the parish.

Another factor that tends to minimize the importance of work with small groups and the amount of time devoted to it is the inclination of both laymen and denominational officials to measure " success " in church programing largely by numerical standards, by the number of people who participate. One of the first questions they ask the minister is: " How many people have been turning out? " Is it any wonder that many ministers are therefore tempted to regard the " Book of Numbers " as a supreme authority and guide in their work, and hence to shy away from work with small groups?

We have also noted how the neglect of small groups has had unfortunate consequences for the work of the minister as pastor-counselor, his ministry to the family unit, and his role as organizer and co-ordinator of the total parish program, particularly in the area of adult education. Are the proportions of time given to the different functions of the ministry to be determined solely by the role expectations projected upon the ministry? Or can we find some determinative standard for a doctrine of the ministry that will transcend the demands of the laity, the larger community, and the promotional pressures exerted by the denominational boards? Are we to minister to our people only as they want or expect to be ministered to? Or shall we seek to emulate Christ's ministry, which went far beyond the people's expectations and altered them? Without some coherent doctrine of the ministry that provides a transcendent standard for ordering and co-ordinating the various roles the minister is to perform, the nature of our ministry will be determined solely by the ideologies and demands of our culture.

H. Richard Niebuhr believes that the present problem is caused by an inability to define the most important activity of the ministry and its one proximate end, around which all other activities and ends may be ordered. He states that " if a new conception of the ministry is emerging, it will be marked by an appearance of a sense of the relative importance of the proximate end sought by the minister in all of them (i.e., in all his roles)," and he defines this proximate end as the increase among men of love for God and for the neighbor.[12]

We can certainly agree with Niebuhr concerning the need for a doctrinal center of focus for the work of the ministry. We can also agree with the proximate end he proposes, the increase among men of love for God and for the neighbor. But it is not proximate *enough;* as a goal, it is too generalized to provide a really practical point of coherence and center of judgment concerning the various functions of the ministry. It is my conviction that the role of the minister as educator, and more particularly as adult educator, deserves priority for both practical and theological reasons, and that it provides a focus of concern which is highly relevant to many of the present problems of the church and its ministry. But before elaborating and evaluating the implications of this conviction for contemporary church life, its theological validity must first be tested.

CHAPTER TWO

A Teaching Ministry and a Teaching Church: Theology

THE MINISTER AS TEACHER

PROTESTANT theology generally speaks of the ministry as " the ministry of the Word." The Bible, as the Word of God, is regarded as the primary source of the minister's authority. Only in a secondary sense does his authority reside in the external fact of being ordained and called to serve by the church. The Word of God is of such central importance for the authority of the Protestant ministry that theologians usually define the apostolic authority of the ministry at least partially in terms of faithfulness to apostolic doctrine and testimony as contained in the Word of God. The insistence upon apostolic succession is not an Anglican peculiarity. Like many of the other theologians of the Reformation, Calvin too believed in apostolic succession as a mark of a valid ministry, at least when defined as a succession in apostolic doctrine. " If the church resides in the successors of the apostles," he writes, " let us search for successors among those only who have faithfully handed their doctrine to posterity. . . . Wherein does the successor consist if it be not in perpetuity of doctrine? " [13]

Daniel Jenkins, a noted Congregational theologian of the twentieth century, likewise argues for the necessity of apostolic succession in terms of faithfulness to apostolic testimony as contained in Scripture. He declares that the ministry is, in essence, a service under the Word of God, a means by which the church is enabled to hear the true Word and to respond to it. The minister is the servant of the church's service of the Word.[14]

Calvin, in his *The Institutes of the Christian Religion,* clearly indicates that the Word is to be regarded as the ultimate basis of the minister's authority:

> When therefore a contemptible mortal, who has just emerged from the dust, addresses us in the name of God, we give the best evidence of our piety and reverence toward God himself, if we readily submit to be instructed by his minister *who possesses no personal superiority to ourselves.* (IV.iii.1.) (Italics mine.)

This same general idea of ministerial authority is reflected in the words of the Genevan Confession of 1537: " Thus we receive the true minister of the Word of God as a messenger and ambassador of God, to whom it is required to hearken as to himself, and we consider their ministry is a commission from God necessary in the Church." Martin Luther, too, was very emphatic in his claims for the divine authority of preaching when it was faithful to the Word of God. In one of his sermons he says: " This is what is meant by ' Thy king cometh.' You do not seek him, but he seeks you. You do not find him, he finds you. For the preachers come from him, not from you." [15]

The Protestant ministry derives its authority from the Word of God; and *the clearest guidance this gives for the ordering of ministerial functions is that those functions are to receive the greatest emphasis which express as fully as possible the reign of the Word of God in the church, and which best facilitate its communication to the people. This central conviction of the Reformation theologians determined the priority they gave to the ministerial functions of preaching and teaching the Word.*

From the time of the Reformation, as James Ainslie has pointed out, the most important work of the minister was preaching. Preaching was a regulative principle of the very nature of the ministry.[16] Even the sacramental authority of the minister was generally derived from his preaching authority. Preaching authorized, authenticated, and interpreted the sacraments. According to Ainslie:

> The prerogative of the minister to be the sole dispenser of the sacraments rests upon the fact that he is the authorized preacher. Preaching is the constituting essential of his office along with which goes the faculty of performing the other most important duties of the ministry as well as lesser duties.[17]

It is interesting to note that in many of the early writings and confessions of the Reformation, such as the Second Helvetic Confession [18] and the Irish Articles of Religion of 1615,[19] the terms "teaching" and "preaching" were used almost interchangeably as synonyms. Many other examples of this tendency virtually to equate the preaching and teaching roles of the ministry could be cited. *The reason for this close relationship between teaching and preaching is to be found in the Reformers' emphasis upon doctrinal and expository preaching.* Wilhelm Pauck reminds us that:

> Early Protestant preaching was doctrinal and became more and more so. . . . It was the goal of the Reformers and of the early Protestant ministry to inculcate right Christian teaching and "pure doctrine" in the minds of men. This is why as *preachers* they were primarily *teachers. The predominance of teaching became apparent also in the general work of the ministry.*[20]

Yet although the Reformers were profoundly aware of the educational values inherent in preaching, they did not regard it as completely adequate in itself for fulfilling the teaching role of the ministry. They felt preaching needed to be supplemented by what they called " private admonition " or " private instruction," although this expression referred at least as much to the instruction of family units as to the instruction of individuals. Zwingli's *The Pastor* stresses that the preaching of repentance must always be followed up by more personal instruction. And Bucer states in his book *The Care of Souls:*

> One must not confine Christian teaching and exhortation to the church service and the pulpit, for there are many who let remain general what is there offered as a general teaching and admonition and who interpret and understand it with respect to others rather than with respect to themselves. Hence it is necessary to instruct the people at home and to give them individual Christian guidance.[21]

Similarly, the 1644 edition of the Presbyterian Directory for the Worship of God declares explicitly that the minister's duties include " private teaching " as well as public teaching through preaching.

Ministers were concerned that the Word of God be individually appropriated according to the specific situations and needs faced by their people; and they were well aware that preaching, by its very nature, lacked this personal specificity. Richard Baxter, for example, regarded preaching as " the most excellent part of the pastor's work "; and yet in *The Reformed Pastor* he repeatedly pointed to the advantages of " private instruction " over preaching if the minister was to " speak to each one's particular necessity." [22] In private, he argued, one may speak more plainly, at the level of each person's understanding. One may utilize repetition and rephrasing where necessary, and one can discover the areas where the layman's knowledge of the faith

needs amplification. Such "private instruction" also en-
ables the layman to understand more fully the message of
the minister's sermons. The teaching role thus complements
the preaching role. Baxter declares:

> I have often been surprised to find how grossly ignorant
> many are who have been my hearers several years, as if
> they had never heard the gospel in their lives. . . . I
> conclude, therefore, that public preaching alone will not
> be sufficient, nor effectual for the conversion of so many
> as this method. Long may you study and preach to little
> purpose, if you neglect this duty.[23]

Doubtless many ministers today who do not carry on any
intensive adult education work in which they could take
soundings of the religious depth of their parishioners would
be as surprised as Baxter was to discover how little of the
gospel their people have appropriated through preaching
alone. The fact that the ministers in Blizzard's survey rated
preaching as most important and teaching as least important
would seem to imply an almost magical belief on their part
in the effectiveness of preaching as a means of fully communicating the Christian gospel without supplementation
by teaching in more personal, face-to-face situations. If
they devoted more attention to personal teaching, as Baxter did, they too would be led to re-evaluate its importance
as an essential supplement to preaching in leading their people toward Christian maturity.

Baxter further strengthens his argument for more personal teaching by citing the example of Christ and the
apostles in the employment of this method of "interlocu-
tory preaching." Whenever they spoke to the people at any
length, he declares, they followed it up with personal discussion.[24] He maintains that this method of "personal instruction" will also serve the important function of informing and awakening the people to an awareness of the true

nature of the ministerial office. Their idea of the ministerial office is often mistakenly confined to the functions of preaching, administering the sacraments, and visiting the sick. They fail to realize that the office of pastoral oversight also includes teaching and counseling, and therefore they often fail to avail themselves of these important pastoral services.

> Show the world, then, by your practice, what the nature of our office is. . . . If they do not know what our office is, viz., that it is one great branch of it to admonish and instruct them with regard to their particular cases, it is no wonder if they neglect to apply to us for our help, to their own prejudice.[25]

Protestantism has traditionally placed a strong emphasis on the religious maturity and understanding of all communicant members. This emphasis is particularly well illustrated in Presbyterianism, although it is by no means confined to it. The Scottish Book of Discipline of 1560 required that at least once a year the minister, together with his elders, was to examine the members of each household in the parish concerning their knowledge of the faith. Those who failed the examination were banned from the Lord's Table until they could pass it.

> For seing that the just levith by his awin faith, and that Christ Jesus justifieth be knawledge off him self, insufferable we judge it that men be permitted to leve and continew in ignorance as memberis of the Churche of God (*sic*).[26]

The main burden of responsibility for preparing for the examinations rested upon the master of each household, and, to a lesser extent, upon his wife. For although the minister was responsible for "private instruction" of the adults together with the catechetical examination of the children, a large part of the teaching role was assigned to the parents. James Smart writes: " In Presbyterian churches the custom continued until the middle of the nineteenth century, and in some quarters still continues, of the minister on his pastoral calls examining the members of the family on their knowledge of the Bible and the catechism, a practice that served to keep parents active, at least in some degree, at their educational task." [27] The minister's work as educator was directed largely toward the *adults* in the family unit. The adults in turn were responsible for preparing the children for the examinations on the catechisms and the Bible which the pastor and the elders administered to them. The main approach to the Christian education of children was thus made through the family unit. Commenting on this family-centered approach, Richard Baxter writes: " If you can thus get masters of families to perform their duty, they will save you much pains with the rest, and greatly promote the success of your labors. *You can not expect a general reformation, till you procure family reformation.*" [28]

Surely, the " family reformation " we should aim at in our churches today, through parent education, should be the awakening of our parents to the fact that the primary responsibility for the Christian nurture of their children rests upon them. They usually regard what efforts they may make in this direction as a supplement to the work of the church school. They should be led to see that the reverse of this should be the case — that the church school should be a secondary supplement to *their* efforts in the home. The " Sabbath school " is a comparatively recent development in Protestantism. It was intended to *supplement* the home as the basic center of Christian nurture, not to *supplant* it. Not only would such a realization on the part of the parents be in accordance with our historic traditions; it would also be in accordance with the obvious fact that the task of Christian education simply cannot be accomplished in the space of one short hour each week. The practical wisdom of the traditional Protestant position is to be seen in the fact that it places the primary responsibility for this task squarely where it belongs — in the home — with the minister's teaching role being directed primarily toward the parents.

We have seen that the primacy of the Word of God in Reformation theology found institutional expression in a primary emphasis on the preaching and teaching of the Word. The Word of God was the major determinant of the authority of the ministry and of the ordering of its functions. Preaching was almost synonymous with teaching, except that the Reformers were acutely aware of the limitations of preaching as a teaching method and therefore encouraged " private instruction " of individuals and families in the parish. In *The Purpose of the Church and Its Ministry*, H. Richard Niebuhr admirably sums up this concept of the primary function of the minister as servant of the Word, as communicator of the gospel:

> Moreover, for the ministers of the Reformed churches " preaching " was a symbolic word; it meant not only public discourse but every action through which men were moved to repent before God and trust in him. Public discourse was never enough; private admonition, catechetical instruction, personal pastoral care, the administration of the sacraments, the leadership of public worship — all these needed to be faithfully attended to; but in everything he did, the preacher had one thing to do, namely, to bring home to men the gospel of divine love.[29]

The traditional Protestant doctrine of the ministry thus was dominated by a unitary principle which gave coherence and meaning and a place on a value scale to every aspect of the minister's work. The minister was a bond servant of the Word of God, not of every passing whim of the people. Yet this ministry was intensely personal, for its chief aim was to make the Word of God understandable and personally relevant to the deepest needs of everyone in the church. As John T. McNeill points out in *The History of the Cure of Souls,* the roles of preacher, teacher, and pastor-counselor were closely integrated by this intense concern for personal relevance.[30] But in the midst of this integration the teaching role remained primary, and in a sense it informed and structured all the other roles. The ministry as the service of the Word meant essentially the communication of the Word; and therefore the teaching role, broadly defined, both included and qualified all the other functions of the ministry.

The Church as Teacher

During the past generation, Christian educators have been making frequent use of the phrase " the teaching church," or " the church as teacher." However, the conception of the nature and function of the church that underlies these phrases is not of recent origin. It is implicit in the conception of the primacy of the teaching and preaching roles of the ministerial office which has been described above, and it can be traced back explicitly to the writings of Calvin and Baxter.

Calvin begins the fourth book of *The Institutes of the Christian Religion,* in which he elaborates his doctrine of the church, by describing the church as a mother and teacher. He abruptly drops the mother metaphor and concentrates his whole attention upon the church as teacher, as a school of doctrine, as a place where men are to be instructed in the ways of the Lord. The primary function of the church is to be a teacher, a disciplinarian, a guardian, a guide. Nor is this teaching function to be confined to children, according to Calvin. Even as adults we can never get beyond the stage of being school children, needing to be disciplined and edified in the faith. He declares:

> Our infirmity will not admit of our dismission from her school; we must continue under her instruction to the end of our lives. . . . We see that God, who might perfect his people in a moment, chooses not to bring them to manhood in any other way than by the education of the church. We see the mode of doing it expressed; the preaching of the heavenly doctrine is committed to pastors. (IV.i.5.)

Here again we see an example of that tendency of the Reformers, noted before, practically to equate preaching and teaching. For Calvin, the church was primarily a teaching church just as its ministry was primarily a teaching ministry. Commenting on this passage, Wilhelm Pauck says that Calvin was speaking of the church as it comes into being through the Word of God, not only as it is preached, but also as it is taught and applied to private and public, individual and social, life. The church becomes the school of Christ through the ministry of the Word. Writes Pauck: " Under the Word of God, therefore, the church is the educator — not by itself, but ' by the instrumentality of men,' the ministers, to whom is assigned ' the preaching of the heavenly doctrine ' and the administration of the whole divine order prescribed by it." [31]

F. W. Dillistone, in his book *The Structure of the Divine Society*, states that the church as a school of Christian doctrine in which everyone, regardless of age, continues to grow in Christian knowledge, was Calvin's ideal. He maintains that this necessarily involved an ideal for the ministry, and that Calvin assumed that the primary if not the sole office of the ministry was to educate the church in the

Biblical faith.[32] This same concept of the church as teacher is echoed over a century later in Baxter's *The Reformed Pastor:* " All Christians are the disciples or scholars of Christ; the church is his school: we are his ushers: the Bible is his grammar: this it is we must be daily teaching them." [33]

CHAPTER THREE

The Centrality of Adult Christian Education

A FOCUS FOR THE MINISTER'S WORK

THE compatibility between traditional Protestant theology and a modern doctrine of the ministry that strongly emphasizes the role of the minister as educator is now evident. Although the theologians of the Reformation did not use the term "adult education" as such, it is clear that they regarded the educating of adults as central to the purpose of the ministry. But the support of tradition is not in itself a sufficient argument for espousing any particular conception of the ministry; it must be tested in terms of its contemporary relevance. We must therefore seek to determine what implications it would have for the present situation of the ministry and the church.

The recovery of the doctrine of the ministry that emerged from the Reformation would first result in upsetting present ministerial preferences and valuations concerning the relative importance of teaching. Instead of being regarded as *least* important and instead of receiving the *smallest* proportion of the minister's time, which Blizzard's survey indicates is the prevailing tendency today, the teaching role would be placed at the top of the list, alongside the preaching role. The present hierarchy of ministerial preferences, with preaching at the top and teaching at the bottom, would become simply untenable for anyone who came to espouse

Protestantism's traditional theological conception of the ministry. Preaching and teaching could not be so radically separated in such a person's mind, either in regard to their relative importance or in regard to their mutual implications for each other.

Repeatedly, those ministers who have carried on an intensive adult education program through small groups testify that they are never short of sermon themes. Much of their preaching grows out of their relationships within these groups, and from the questions and problems posed in these groups by their laymen. Their teaching and preaching roles mutually reinforce each other, they declare, whenever the content of their preaching is related to the content of discussion in these groups. This helps to make their preaching more relevant. It also serves as a means for testing how well they communicate through their preaching. These men have discovered for themselves the validity of the intimate connection between *kerygma* and *didache*, the proclamation of the gospel and the teaching of it, which is maintained in the New Testament.

The Reformers, as we have seen, placed great emphasis on doctrinal and expository preaching because they regarded the ministry of preaching as an integral part of the more inclusive ministry of teaching. The contemporary revival of doctrinal and expository preaching would receive an even greater impetus if this insight of the Reformers into the interrelatedness of teaching and preaching were recovered. Of course, this kind of preaching is, at its best, never purely didactic. But by means of such preaching, the minister who is aware of the supportive relationship that exists between his roles as preacher and teacher will always seek to instruct as well as to inspire. Also, he will seek to develop many types of church programing that will combine these two roles creatively. While I was serving as assistant pastor in a church in Yonkers, New York, the minister and I decided, with the enthusiastic support of the session, to depart from the traditional, stereotyped midweek service during Lent, a service that scarcely differed from a Sunday morning service. Together we preached a series of Lenten sermons, one year on the historical events of Passion Week, another year on troublesome phrases in the Apostles' Creed. The services were shortened to provide time for a discussion period, which we called the " After-Word," immediately following each service. A majority of the worshipers stayed and met together in small discussion groups which provided opportunities for further exploration and development of the ideas presented in the sermons.

For a number of years, Gerald J. Jud, pastor of the First Congregational Church of West Haven, Connecticut, has been conducting an even more creative Lenten program. His congregation is organized into neighborhood groups called " colonies." The series of Lenten sermons he preaches are mimeographed, and each sermon is distributed on the Sunday it is delivered. The content of the sermon provides the basis for discussion when the colony groups gather in the homes during the following week. Thus, the message of the sermon is not only heard, but also read, reflected upon, and discussed.

These are but two examples of how preaching and teaching can be directly combined in the program of adult education. The possibilities for other variations are almost limitless. But regardless of whether or not a minister deliberately chooses to combine teaching and preaching in the parish program in such an organized manner, he will find that they will mutually reinforce each other as a means of communicating the Christian gospel.

The recovery of the Reformation doctrine of the ministry would also help clarify the complementary relationship that can exist between the role of the minister as educator and his role as pastor-counselor, and it could enable him to function more effectively in each. An understanding of the potentially therapeutic and preventive psychological by-products of adult education through small groups would help the minister in utilizing such groups to augment his efforts to help his people attain personality integration through individual counseling. Furthermore, it would contribute to his own personal sense of wholeness amidst the many roles he must perform. Dr. Jud, whose unique Lenten program was cited above, states that he is very grateful for a small, intimate women's study group in his church which he uses to help long-term counselees find a place of meaningful fellowship in the life of the church. He sees clearly the supportive relationship between his role as adult educator and his role as pastor-counselor:

> So the ministry of our church to those in crisis is two-pronged. As pastor I utilize the best counseling technique I know to help those in trouble, providing a relationship wherein they may face honestly their true condition and mediating forgiveness and acceptance. The church provides in the small groups loving community wherein acceptance and forgiveness and the sense of belonging may increasingly be experienced, and where the individual may have opportunity for continued growth and development in the Christian life.[34]

In the first chapter, the suggestion was made that the counseling load of many ministers could be made lighter if they were aware of how study groups might supplement the processes of individual guidance and counseling. Howard B. Haines, pastor of the First Presbyterian Church of Middletown, New York, bears out the truth of this observation as he evaluates the influence of the small groups he helped develop:

In many cases, the group takes up where the individual counseling leaves off, supplementing it or even eliminating it entirely. I have been repeatedly thankful that a group was available to give steady guidance to a person who had made a fresh start in Christian living, but who still had a long way to go. This has been especially true in cases of loneliness, moderate emotional instability, inability to understand others, and need of continued guidance in the use of prayer and the Bible and the accepting and giving of love. In the nature of the case no amount of individual counseling can fully deal with these needs. The "priesthood of all believers" becomes a realized fact, with each person helping to open up for his neighbor the way to God.[35]

Doubtless, many people have been helped to a more creative psychological adjustment through a combination of private counseling sessions with the minister together with membership in a study group, without the minister being conscious of the supportive connection between the two. But if he had a conception of the ministry that included a conscious awareness of the close complementary relationship between teaching and counseling, he would be able to utilize the church's study groups even more effectively, thus providing many of his counselees with help he alone could not give them.

Because such a large proportion of a minister's personal counseling work involves problems that center around the area of family relationships, he should be particularly aware of the part that parent education groups can play in supporting his counseling role. But quite aside from this important consideration, a recovery of the traditional Protestant principle of directing one's teaching ministry primarily toward the family unit would in itself lead the minister to place a stronger emphasis on the Christian education of the parents of his church school children.

One of the best features of the new Seabury curriculum of the Protestant Episcopal Church is its approach to Christian education through the family unit and its stress on parent education. Family worship services are integral to the functioning of this curriculum, and parents' classes, relating theology to family life situations, are a requirement for parishes using it. A series of six books, published prior to the publication of the curriculum itself, are for the reference and general reading of the adults of the church. They represent a comprehensive outline of the church's theology, traditions, and practices. The content of the Christian faith is to be transmitted primarily through family worship and the education of the adults who are, in turn, the parents and teachers in the church.

No other denominational curriculum provides such a comprehensive family-centered educational program as this. But churches of other denominations would do well to emulate this emphasis on family worship services and family night programs. In addition, they can select materials for the adult church school class that parallel in content the curriculum of the children's classes and that deal with family life problems. In this way, the Sunday morning adult church school class could become, in effect, a parents class, without alienating the " old faithfuls," who are usually satisfied so long as the content of their material is Biblical and theological. For the parents of church school children, relating Christian doctrine to family living would touch on their immediate interests and concerns. For the others in the class, the insertion of family life problems into the discussion would not be at all irrelevant, but would serve to illustrate theological affirmations in terms of common human relationships. The minister who thus expands the traditional adult church school class into a parents class, or classes, which is more obviously functional and inclusive in its appeal to adult concerns, will be taking an important step toward providing family-centered Christian education. Not only will he be helping parents to utilize the resources of the Christian faith in solving problems of family life; he will also be helping parents equip themselves with the curricular content essential for coherent religious discussion in the home, discussion that will complement the work of the church school teachers.

A recovery of the historic Protestant emphasis on the teaching function of the ministry would also help to integrate and clarify the relationship between the roles of teacher and priest (i.e., the role of leading in public worship and administering the sacraments). Lewis J. Sherrill reminds us that the reading of Scripture in public worship originated as an act of teaching in both Jewish synagogue worship and in Christian services. The reading was primarily for the purpose of instructing the religious community by confronting it with the Word of God. Thus it was common to the genius of both the Jewish and the Christian community to embed teaching in their corporate worship.[36]

A minister who is aware of both the historical and the practical relationship between his roles as priest and as teacher would be likely to prepare his congregation for understanding the reading of Scripture in public worship by frequently making some explanatory comments as an introduction. Both in theory and in practice, he would maintain a close connection between his *priestly* function in the administration of the Lord's Supper and Baptism and his *prophetic* function as preacher, interpreting the written Word which validates and authenticates the sacraments as the " enacted Word." His is the ministry of the Word *and* the sacraments, and he would not discharge these functions as though they were quite unrelated. The language of faith, as it is found in our orders for the sacraments of Baptism and the Lord's Supper and in the classic prayers we use, often falls upon the ears of the people as an alien tongue. The minister's teaching and preaching support his priestly function when they are used to translate and interpret the church's liturgical language in terms the layman can understand.

A view of the ministry that emphasizes the teaching function would result, also, in a new evaluation of the role of the minister as organizer. It would awaken the minister to a realization of the opportunities for adult Christian education inherent in the meetings of small official groups in the church. He would seek in all of these meetings not merely the efficient execution of the business at hand, nor even simply to train his officers for the more efficient performance of their particular duties; he would seek to awaken them to a fuller recognition of their stewardship and of the function of their offices in relation to the mission and purpose of the church. In program-planning groups he would play the role of resource person, and also, perhaps, the role of Socratic gadfly, leading the planners to consider the purpose of their organization and its relation to the purpose of the church as this institution seeks the way of obedient service to the Word of God. He would lead them to address themselves to the question: Are our activities on the periphery or at the heart of the profoundest human concerns? Lay leaders in programing must be equipped with an adequate doctrine of the church, its ultimate goals and purposes, before they can adequately evaluate the content of their programs.

A related result of this new attitude toward the roles of the minister as educator and organizer would surely be a lessening of the proportion of time now spent in the role of administrator. We noted earlier that for nearly all the min-

isters in Blizzard's survey the role of parish administrator
was the most time-consuming of all. They spent an amaz-
ingly large amount of their time each week in mimeograph-
ing, typing, filing, etc., not to mention other aspects of
parish administration. It seems reasonable to assume that one
of the chief reasons for this is the failure of the minister as
educator and organizer to train his lay officers as capable
administrators. Many of the respondents in Blizzard's survey
wrote that they could not see any great difference between
their administrative work and the work of the average layman in the business world.

The irony of this situation is that the average minister
spends the greatest block of his time performing a role for
which many of his lay people would be as well or even better qualified than he. Not only does this represent poor
stewardship of his special talents and training; it also deprives many of his laymen of a means of essential Christian
service for which they are well suited. If " curriculum " is
defined as all those experiences which are a part of Christian
growth and change, then certainly administrative service to
the church is an important part of the adult curriculum.
Large segments of the minister's administrative load could
be carried by laymen with a minimum of instruction
through church officer training — provided, of course, that
the minister sees to it that their theological grounding is
sufficient to preserve a saving tension between the secular
presuppositions of the business community and the theological presuppositions of the church.

Quite aside from the actual training of church officers in
the work of parish administration, the minister who properly fulfills his role as educator in a general adult program
will derive from this *indirect* benefits in the reduction of
his administrative load. Carl R. Smith and Robert W. Lynn,
ministers of the Montview Boulevard Presbyterian Church

in Denver, admit that it is a time-consuming task for the minister to be the leader of adult study groups. However, one of the major justifications they give for this expenditure of time and energy is their own experience that "these groups have provided a source of potential church leaders, officers who know something of the faith of the church as well as how to run a financial campaign." [37] Surely, one important compensation that offsets the new demands placed on the minister's time by the development of study groups in the church is the emergence of willing and devoted lay people, leaders who will assume many administrative responsibilities that the minister presently has to carry himself because his laymen are too unprepared or too lightly committed. Study groups that bring lay people to a deeper understanding of the Bible and the meaning of the Christian faith, and to a fuller comprehension of the meaning of church membership, can function as a seedbed for potential lay leadership.

One important ministerial function not dealt with in Blizzard's study is the role of evangelist, a role that has always embodied the very essence of the ministry. Here again, the close relationship between education and evangelism is evident, even though one rejects the virtual equation of the two propounded by many liberal Protestant educational theorists of a generation ago. The relationship between the roles of the minister as educator and as evangelist becomes clear not only in connection with his work with adult communicants classes and inquirers groups, but also in his work with official groups and every kind of voluntary group wherein he endeavors to prepare his laymen to be coherent, articulate witnesses among those outside the church.

Such groups, provided they have a permissive atmosphere conducive to free discussion, can provide laymen with opportunities for verbalizing their faith. Unless they have had opportunity to communicate their Christian convictions to other committed Christians, they cannot be expected to communicate them convincingly to those outside the church. To send out lay visitation teams into the homes of the unchurched or semichurched without their previously having had this kind of experience in sharing their faith is as irresponsible an act as enlisting new church school teachers and then not training them. When Jesus sent his twelve disciples out on an evangelistic mission, he said to them, " Behold, I send you out as sheep in the midst of wolves " (Matt. 10:16, RSV); but these "sheep" had been thoroughly trained and instructed beforehand by him so that they might be " wise as serpents." Christ's ministers should do the same for those members of their flock who carry on lay visitation.

Unquestionably our current weakness in the area of evangelism can, to a considerable extent, be attributed to the failure of the ministry to inform the laity adequately concerning the essentials of Biblical theology, Christian doctrine, and church history. Education is certainly not identical with evangelism; but a recovery by the ministry of an awareness to the central importance of the teaching role is essential if our laymen are to be equipped for the task of evangelism that the Christian gospel lays upon them as well as upon us.

Each year the ministerial market is glutted with new pamphlets and books and articles in the field of practical theology, stressing one or another aspect of the minister's work. The minister is admonished to spend more time on evangelism, or preaching, or pastoral counseling, or liturgics, or any one of a number of other facets of his office that happens to be the writer's pet concern. The common reaction is to say to oneself: " Yes, I should give more attention to that area of my work. But where in the world am I to find the time? " Such admonitions are not particularly helpful. These moralistic appeals only add to the minister's sense of confusion amidst all his functions, and to his feeling of guilt and frustration as he labors under almost intolerable pressures. The minister is as much interested in knowing how he may *subtract* time from some of his functions as he is in deciding where to *add* time to others. Without a unifying principle to help him understand his ministry, he will only add and subtract in passive response to the dominant role expectations projected upon him.

A doctrine of the ministry that stresses the teaching role above all, and that nevertheless is able to relate all other ministerial roles to the teaching role in a way that clarifies their significance, provides the minister with a core of professional integrity and coherence in the light of which all his various functions may be seen and evaluated. By means of such a conception of the work of the ministry he may seek to transform the role expectations of his laymen instead of being simply submissive to them. It is not so much a matter of the minister spending more time at his work as it is a matter of redistributing his time among his various roles in terms of this new priority.

If he is aware of the complementary relationship between the teaching role and the preaching role, he will realize that the study he devotes to preparing himself for adult group leadership reinforces his preaching as well, and that many sermon ideas will come directly out of the group experience itself. By seeing the potentially complementary relationship between the teaching role and the organizational and administrative roles, he will be able to decrease the amount of time spent on the administrative role by increasing the amount of time spent on the teaching and organizational roles. Through a more extensive and intensive program of church officer training and through the recruitment of persons who have come to a fuller commitment through experience in other study groups, he would decrease his administrative load in the name of the ministry of the laity. At the same time, he would increase his participation in the area of organizational activities by functioning more responsibility as an educational adviser and resource person. Thus, both extremes of ministerial domination in the area of parish administration and ministerial laissez faire in the area of parish organization would be moderated toward more truly democratic leadership in each. Such a view of the ministry, particularly as it is reinforced by a realization of the complementary relationship between the teaching and counseling roles, would result in an increased sense of the importance of ministering to small groups within the church.

In his book *The Purpose of the Church and Its Ministry*, H. Richard Niebuhr seems to be suggesting some such order of priority among the functions of the ministry in his conception of the minister as what he calls the " pastoral director." His ultimate standard of judgment for the work of the ministry is, as we have seen, the increase among men of love for God and for the neighbor; his intermediate standard of judgment is the presentation of the gospel; and his most specific standard of judgment is the " edification " of the church. Expressed in somewhat different terms, these are also the criteria of Protestant theology in general and of the view of the teaching ministry I would propose as a cornerstone for reformulating a relevant doctrine of the ministry.

Commenting on the work of the " pastoral director," as he pictures it, Niebuhr declares that it will include all the traditional functions of the ministry, such as preaching, leading in public worship and administering the sacraments, counseling, and presiding over the organizational life of the church; but these functions are to be ordered in a special way. " His first function," states Niebuhr, " is that of building or ' edifying ' the church; he is concerned in everything that he does to bring into being a people of God who as a church will serve the purpose of the church in the local community and the world." [38] His work is centered upon guiding the church to become a means for increasing among men the love of God and neighbor. The church is to become a corporate ministry of reconciliation, and the minister is to function as its servant, directing it in its service of reconciliation. In his role as preacher, the " pastoral director " seeks to instruct, to persuade, and to counsel persons who need to grow in their understanding of the meaning of the Christian faith so that they can interpret it to others. Therefore, his preaching will be Biblical in the more inclusive sense of the word, and it will be related organically to his functions as educator and pastoral counselor, and to the evangelistic function of the entire church.[39]

Concerning the role of the " pastoral director " as pastor-counselor and educator, Niebuhr goes on to say:

> The activity on behalf of individuals is for this pastoral director not only a matter of pastoral rule or of the pastoral care of souls, though it will include both, but is best designated as pastoral counseling, a counseling that has them in view as needing reconciliation to God but also to men. . . . So also as teacher, the pastoral director becomes the teacher of teachers, the head of all educational organization which he cannot simply manage but must lead as a competent Christian educator.[40]

The minister as pastor-counselor, seeking to lead people toward reconciliation with their fellows as well as with God, will utilize the possibilities for personal reconciliation that small study groups uniquely afford. And as the " teacher of teachers," whether these are church school teachers, adult program planners, or parents, he accomplishes what he neither can nor should accomplish by himself. Implicit in the idea of the " priesthood of all believers " is the idea that the task of Christian education is the task of all the adult members of the church. It is the function of the minister to prepare them for this task.

Staff Ministries and Adult Education

It is inevitable that in larger churches there should be some degree of specialization as to ministerial roles. In very large churches we find such extremes of specialization as pastoral counselors, parish callers, and occasionally an ordained parish administrator. Much more commonly, we find a division of responsibility in which a director of Christian education or an assistant minister is primarily responsible for the youth work and children's work. Their job descriptions may include work with communicants classes or other adult study groups.

In churches that carry on an extensive program of adult education, these educational assistants almost invariably have a part in it. Where there is no such extensive program, they may often awaken the interest of the senior minister and of the rest of the adult congregation through truly creative teacher-training groups that become enthusiastically spoken of throughout the parish. Where teacher-training is essentially confined to training in teaching methods, this is not likely to happen. However, it can and has happened in instances where these groups are led to discuss the content of the church school curriculum not only in terms of its relevance to the children, but also in terms of its relevance to the teachers themselves. Parents classes, often led by the educational assistant, can also serve as a starting point for wider interest in adult education.

However, there is one danger the educational assistant

must keep in mind. Several experimenters in the field of group dynamics have pointed out that in intimate, face-to-face groups in their early stages of development a special type of relationship often develops between some of the members and the group leader. This relationship is similar to that which often develops between patient and analyst during the process of psychoanalysis, a relationship that the analysts refer to as the " transference phenomenon." It is characterized by strong feelings of dependence, bordering on infatuation, which the patient has toward the analyst. This " transference phenomenon " can occur between the members of a group and its leader, even though it is not as pronounced or obvious in the dynamics of small groups as it is in psychoanalysis. In both cases, it represents an immature state of development which gives way to independence and greater personality integration when the personal interactions are guided by a skillful analyst or group leader.

But this phenomenon, whenever it develops in a group, can present the educational assistant as group leader with a great temptation which is nothing short of demonic. The senior minister usually receives most of the congregation's adulation; and here is a ready-made opportunity for the educational assistant to gratify his own egoistic needs by having a small group of people who are very closely attached to him because of this group experience. Dissident laymen, who for one reason or another dislike the senior minister, may gravitate toward a group led by the educational assistant, and their antipathy toward the one may grow apace with their affection for the other. Some degree of professional jealousy, disagreement, and personal friction exists within every church staff arrangement, and this heightens the temptation which this situation may hold for the educational assistant. He must exercise every precaution lest the group become emotionally ingrown or, even worse, a potentially divisive influence in the loyalty of its members. As servant of the Word of God, his task is to lead the group beyond an immature attraction to and dependence upon him. He must arouse, instead, an attraction to and dependence upon the Word he is called to communicate.

There are, of course, many quite legitimate advantages and satisfactions that come to an educational assistant through intensive work with adults. He seldom has as many competent and committed church school teachers and youth advisers as he would like to have. Obviously, the leadership training he conducts is important; but work with communicants classes, parents discussion groups, and the like can go even farther toward meeting the church's needs for educational leadership by stimulating other adults to commit themselves to official responsibilities in the church's ministry to children and youth. Such groups provide the educational assistant with opportunities for enlisting new coworkers in his educational task. Furthermore, since the educational assistant usually preaches only occasionally if at all, he is not likely to feel the need for disciplined study which the weekly preaching responsibility demands. Leadership responsibility in one or more adult study groups imposes a valuable discipline for his own intellectual and spiritual growth and the enrichment of his ministry.

A senior minister is fortunate indeed if he has such an assistant to aid him in the church's program of adult education. However, he should not succumb to the temptation of overspecialization by consigning all the adult education work in the church to his educational assistant. The reciprocal reinforcement that can exist between the roles of the minister as educator and as preacher and pastor-counselor is an advantage that would be lost if the senior minister were to abdicate his teaching function. He and his educational assistant should work together in the church's program of adult education, as a means of achieving greater satisfaction and effectiveness in all their many functions. It is their task together, as adult educators, to enable the church to teach.

A Redefinition of the Church as Teacher

The Reformation emphasis on the teaching function of the ministry was based upon a conception of the church's primary purpose as teacher, which was to serve as a vehicle for the communication of the Word. So likewise, a contemporary definition of the ministry as essentially a teaching order (implied, for example, in the ordination of Presbyterian ministers as " teaching elders ") must be based on a rediscovery of the significance of the church as teacher. There must be a recovery of the Reformers' conviction that the teaching function of the church as a whole is absolutely essential to its very nature. Even though, as in New Testament times, only certain members hold specific teaching offices, the responsibility for teaching rests upon the whole church. It is as much the duty of the entire church as is the hearing of the Word and participation in the sacraments. Indeed, it is the proper response of the church to the Word and the sacraments.

To regard the church as primarily a teacher is not to minimize the importance of its functions as an evangelistic, witnessing, worshiping, and reconciling community, any more than regarding the minister as primarily an educator minimizes the importance of his other functions; rather, it means subsuming all these other functions of the church under the unifying category of the communication of the gospel. The communication of the gospel is the crowning theological category of which every proper activity of the church is a part, and constitutes the apostolic obligation of the church. The church as communicator of the gospel, as God's chief agent of continuing revelation, is a teaching

church. Any ministry is defective if it is not, in large measure, a teaching ministry; and a teaching ministry is defective if it does not bear fruit in a teaching church. In nearly
every instance, the adult education program of the church
must be initiated by the minister. But his goal as adult educator is to make every adult in his church an educator,
whether that adult be a parent, a church school teacher, or a
leader among other adults, in order that the ideal of a teaching church may become a reality.

The traditional Protestant emphasis on the church as
teacher, and its correlative emphasis on the teaching ministry, finds contemporary support in the growing recognition that the church *inevitably* and unavoidably teaches and
communicates definite meanings. Education of some sort
goes on where there is any activity in the church. This
principle was recognized years ago in the statement in the
International Curriculum Guide concerning adult Christian
education. According to this statement, the curriculum of
adult education consists of all the activities the church provides, uses, or recognizes for guiding the growth of persons
in their relationship to God, the church, other persons, and
themselves. Therefore worship, preaching, study groups,
service enterprises, social fellowship, social action, and even
recreation are included in this broad concept of Christian
education for adults. It may be argued fairly that we cannot
choose, within this inclusive definition, whether or not we
ought to conduct a program of " adult education " in the
church; we can only choose what *kind* of " adult education " we should have.

The things that are taught, the meanings that are communicated, are conditioned to a great extent by the quality
of the personal relationships that exist within the fellowship of the church. The church communicates its faith to
all those with whom it has contact through the quality of

the personal interactions within its fellowship, i.e., through relationships in worship, work, study, and recreational activity. This kind of " teaching " goes on irrespective of what is said or not said from the pulpit, in the study course, or in the lecture series. It either contradicts or reinforces what is taught verbally in the more formalized educational activities of the church. Something is always being communicated to people through the social environment of the church, whether consciously directed through formal effort or as a result of the impact and influence of persons upon one another. A satisfactory modern view of the church as teacher thus must define " teaching " and " communication " in the broadest possible sense.

In this regard, the contemporary emphasis that Christian educators place on the church as teacher both affirms and transcends the historic Protestant conception of the church as teacher. The traditional view fully recognized the educational aspect of every major formal function of the church and its ministry. But the tendency was to regard the communication of the gospel as essentially a verbal matter, rather than as something intimately related to the field of interpersonal relationships, something that can and does occur outside the use of verbal symbols. The ministry of the Word, in short, was defined too literally as a ministry of words. According to Hendrik Kraemer:

> The extravagant and nearly exclusive stress on verbal communication, on preaching and sermonizing, in the world of the churches, which issued from the Reformation, was a degeneration or distortion of the Reformers' rediscovery of the prophetic character and quality of the Word of God. This stress has closed the eyes of the church to the manifold means of communication which we find in the Bible, which in contradiction to our Western world is not confined to, or imprisoned in, a " verbal

culture." . . . The Christian message, which must be communicated, has such deep and wide dimensions that they transcend the territory of verbal culture, howsoever refined and high its standard may be.[41]

Yet the assumption that teaching is done primarily through verbal communication still seems to be quite common among ministers. Back of this assumption lies another one: that words have absolute and intrinsic meanings within themselves. Actually, very few significant and profound words have identical meanings for all people. When people use or hear the important words of our faith, the meaning they attach to them varies greatly, for the meaning of the words has been individually forged out of the raw material of previous experiences of personal relationship. The words that constitute the vocabulary of the Christian faith arose out of historical experiences of relationship between God, man, and society, and they can be apprehended only on the basis of contemporary experiences of relationship.

The church in its teaching function has put too much faith in the use of words and has paid too little attention to what Reuel Howe calls the "language of relationships," which conditions and determines the personal meaning of words. As a result, people are not helped to understand the theological meanings of their personal relationships within and outside the fellowship of the church, or helped to bring these meanings to the understanding of the words used in preaching and other methods of formal teaching.

Secular educators have been reminding us for years that words have both logical (objective) and psychological (subjective) meanings. The church as teacher provides both types of meanings: logical meanings through the words the church uses and psychological meanings through the personal relationships that exist between its members.

The church must give a great amount of attention to the quality of the relationship experiences of its people if the psychological meanings of the terminology of the faith are to support and not negate the logical meanings.

Thus, contemporary expressions of the idea of the church as teacher go even beyond the insights of the Reformation, in that they recognize the educational implications contained in human relations. One of the greatest weaknesses of the earlier post-Reformation churches and their ministry in exercising the teaching function was an excessive verbalism, with which was associated an arid and authoritarian dogmatism which in many ways failed to make contact with the emotional dimensions of human experience. Teaching was regarded essentially as " telling "; its common synonyms were " admonishing," " instructing," " rebuking," and the like. There was a tendency to define religious knowledge as the memorization of Biblical facts and passages and of precisely worded catechetical answers to theological questions posed only by the catechisms themselves. The teaching role of the ministry was directed toward the family unit, and the family's opportunity and responsibility for Christian education was fully recognized. Yet there was a general neglect of other possible primary groupings as important agents for Christian nurture.

A new formulation of the idea of the church as teacher, which takes the interpersonal dimension of human experience more fully into account, can overcome these limitations of the Protestant tradition. A philosophy of Christian adult education based on this new formulation will necessarily direct greater attention to the quality of interpersonal relations in parish life. To this end, a minister sharing this philosophy will foster within the parish the development of small study groups in which the language of relationships may support the spoken Word.

A doctrinal conviction of the primacy of the teaching function of the church and its ministry can restore wholeness to the minister's understanding of his work and a basis of coherence for the total program of the parish. Blizzard's study, together with an observation of the purposelessness and unrelatedness of both people and activities which seem to be all too typical of many parishes, indicates the need for such a unitary principle. The particular conception of the church and its ministry that has been argued here is no panacea for all the problems that beset the church and the ministry in our time; but at least it provides a practical theological point of reference for the hard work needed to solve them.

CHAPTER FOUR

The Layman: Today

ONCE the minister has arrived at some degree of self-understanding concerning his primary mission and the relation of all his roles to this central goal, it is important for him to deepen his understanding of the laymen toward whom his teaching ministry is directed. It is imperative that a relevant philosophy of adult Christian education include some grasp of their central needs and problems. Obviously, the outline of such a philosophy cannot hope to include all the important and pertinent data that sociology, psychology, and theology have to offer toward an understanding of the layman. Nevertheless, if it is to be truly relevant, such a philosophy must reflect an awareness of the salient contributions these disciplines can make toward the illumination of the layman's situation. Without such an awareness, the church and its ministry are likely to proclaim answers to questions that the layman's contemporary life situation does not directly pose, answers that therefore will be peripheral or even wholly irrelevant to the needs of the average layman.

It may indeed be argued that there is no such thing as "the average layman": that the situation of each layman is unique, and that in a pluralistic society like ours such generalizations are meaningless. However, it is fair to say that members of the "great American middle class" of skilled and semiskilled commercial and industrial workers and professional people do, in fact, have in common a large area of problems which are definable by sociologists and other perceptive observers of American society and which the adult education program of the church can and must make relevant to these problems. The situation of the layman in rural America is, of course, somewhat different, but not sufficiently different to warrant separate treatment here; for the rapid expansion of urban and suburban culture and folkways into the rural areas of this country continually lessens these differences.

In the area of psychological problems that are generally associated with the various age ranges within the adult spectrum, or that are symptomatic of contemporary American culture in general, even greater generalization is permissible. And in the next chapter, in the area of theological investigation, where man is seen as man-before-God, we can speak of the universal and perennial predicaments of man. But the purpose of every sociological, psychological, or theological generalization concerning our laymen will be to aid us in discovering its practical implications for the ultimate task of adult Christian education, which is to mediate through the church and its ministry God's redeeming answers to man's deepest needs.

THE TREND TOWARD " OTHER-DIRECTEDNESS "

A number of observers of the American scene have become increasingly aware, in recent years, of the great manipulative pressures toward conformity that are being exerted on men and women in every area of life. In *The Courage to Be*, Paul Tillich speaks of a gradual trend in American life toward what he calls " neoconformism," in which people seek to solve the riddles and anxieties of existence through the " courage-to-be-as-a-part." In his recent book *The Organization Man,* William H. Whyte vividly portrays this tendency as he observes it in the middle and upper echelons of the business community, both in the downtown office and in Exurbia. His devastating indictment of the " engineering of consent " and the shaping of men into conforming automatons through the manipulative use of group dynamics and the " science of human relations " by the top managerial levels reveals a sensitivity toward the demonic potentialities of the " science " of group dynamics which is often lacking in the enthusiastic literature of adult education workers today.

Probably the most penetrating analysis of this problem of conformity has been presented by David Riesman in *The Lonely Crowd.* Riesman maintains that within recent generations there has been a general shift in American personality type from a predominance of what he calls " inner-directedness " to a predominance of what he calls " other-directedness." The selfhood of the inner-directed man is determined largely by principles and ideals implanted in his youth. In contrast with this, the other-directed man's personality and world view are determined largely by his contemporaries, both those directly known to him and those with whom he is indirectly acquainted through friends and through the mass media. His goals and values shift according to the guidance given by verbal and visual " signals " from others. Thus his conformity is not limited to the externals of appearance and propriety, but also involves his values and attitudes and all that is most intimately bound up with his selfhood.

The other-directed person, according to Riesman, primarily seeks adjustment in life. He seeks to have the character that is expected of him, and even the inner experiences and emotions, as well as the outward behavior, that are expected to go with it. He does not desire fame, but only the respect and affection of the jury of his peers that constantly judges him. The role expectations projected on him by his peers and superiors, and by the reference groups toward which he is directed, are internalized as his personal goals and ideals. The minister will be better able to understand his laymen in this regard if he has sufficient perception to recognize the degree to which his own personality structure tends to be other-directed in the same way — his temptation to define himself largely in terms of the role expectations his laymen have concerning his work.

Upward social mobility is, of course, one of the guiding and insatiable dreams of the middle class. For the other-directed person, social and economic advancement seems to depend less on what he is and does than on what others think of him and how competent he is at manipulating others and in allowing himself to be manipulated. Riesman says that "*the product now in demand is neither a staple nor a machine; it is a personality*." [42] William H. Whyte speaks of the " commercial valuation of personality traits " as determined by the personality tests used by the personnel departments of the big companies,[43] and C. Wright Mills in *White Collar* refers to the business community as " The Personality Market," " The Great Salesroom " where the chief commodity offered for rent by the average white-collar worker is his personality.[44]

The manipulative element in personal interaction is stressed by all these writers. Both economic and emotional security and fulfillment are sought through the manipulation of the self and of others in this milieu of other-directedness. From a sampling of a group of women's magazines on which he made a content analysis, Riesman concludes that " a good many stories and features and, of course far less subtly, many ads, dealt largely with modes of manipulating the self in order to manipulate others, primarily for the attainment of intangible assets such as affection." [45]

Riesman, Mills, Whyte, and others feel strongly that we are living in a culture in which social relationships are essentially instrumental and manipulative, rather than ends in themselves. Writes Riesman:

> Obliged to conciliate or manipulate a variety of people, the other-directed person handles all men as customers who are always right; but he must do this with the realization that, as Everett Hughes has put it, some are more right than others. This diversity of roles to be taken with a diversity of customers is not institutionalized or clear-cut, and the other-directed person tends to become merely his succession of roles and encounters and hence to doubt who he is and where he is going.[46]

The question " Who am I? " thus becomes highly relevant for the layman caught up in the " Personality Market." Just who is he, aside from the succession of masks he wears and the parts he acts out both in his work and in his leisure? His is the " anxiety of nonbeing," to use Tillich's phrase. His self-identity is threatened. The personality patterns expected of him often mean that he must manipulate others as if they were objects rather than persons, and he in turn must submit to the same treatment in the name of success and security and acceptance by others. He has the anxiety-producing problem of combining the appearances of friendly, personalized, " sincere " behavior with the ruthless, sometimes almost paranoid, rivalries and envies of his occupational life. Lewis J. Sherrill ably sums up the condition of mass man, imprisoned in this manipulative, other-directed nightmare:

> Again, the existing self may not be able to attain liberation. For whatever reason, he finds himself dominated. The domination may be exerted by other persons, or by institutions, or by vast impersonal forces outside himself,

against which he feels himself powerless. He feels himself being manipulated and resents it, resents the persons
or forces that manipulate him, and resents himself for
allowing himself to be manipulated; and yet can find no
way to break out from under the domination. He then
may find that he must hide the resentment and "play
the game" for stakes which, if he wins them, only bind
him more securely in the bondage which he inwardly
loathes.[47]

Now obviously, it is nearly impossible either to prove or
to disprove the accuracy of such generalizations concerning the personality structure of our laymen. Their utility
lies in their validity as profiles, as generalizations which
ring true to our own observations and experiences. Such
statements are descriptive rather than scientific. They are
based on insights rather than on measurements. But the
truth of these assertions concerning a tendency toward
greater conformity at all levels of life, toward increasing
other-directedness and manipulation in social relationships,
is surely validated experientially by our own perceptions.

These pressures toward conformity inherent in our culture greatly heighten the leverage that the practice of the
principles of group dynamics may have upon the individual.
The power of the adult group leader in the church to
change people's attitudes and beliefs and values through
group dynamics techniques has been considerably increased by this social tendency toward other-directedness.
Of course, this power may be exercised either creatively or
destructively. It may be employed as a means of fostering
genuine encounter between laymen and the sharing of
ideas, and as a means of increasing personality integration
through this interaction. On the other hand, it may become
a means of violating the integrity of the individual, his right
to say no as well as yes and his right to independent self-

hood, through a manipulative approach that treats people as objects. An aggressive, doctrinaire leader can use some of the principles of group dynamics to manipulate others toward a consensus that is not genuine, toward an external conformity to ideas that cloaks a suppressed hostility toward the ideas and other members of the group.

But on the positive side, the small group, functioning as a fellowship of genuine concern, may be employed as a means of answering the needs of the other-directed for approval and acceptance. Furthermore, it may easily become an important reference group of peers for its members because the convictions and insights concerning the gospel and the gospel's implications for the common life that become a matter of group consensus will be quickly internalized and personally appropriated by the other-directed individual. This internalizing of the gospel provides a source for that inner-directedness in thought and action which the other-directed individual so sorely needs.

In terms of content for adult Christian education, the problems of other-directedness point toward a need for emphasis on the Biblical theme of God's providence as the answer to the predicament of man as he feels himself caught in the clutches of ruthless and impersonal forces external to him in all his social relationships. Christian teachings concerning the nature of man and of Christian love are also relevant to the layman's need for a basis of self-understanding and for an inner-directed ethic which transcends the manipulative ethic of his social environment.

However, a *direct* approach to these Christian themes and doctrines may utterly fail to have any redemptive value, because they may be the answers to questions that the layman has not yet been led to ask or to problems of which he is not yet consciously aware. As Robert Lynn and Robert Spike [48] have suggested, the utilization of con-

temporary literature for group study as a means of illumi-
nating the predicament of man in a mass society may help
bring these largely unrealized and unconscious problems to
a conscious level. Then the Word of God can speak to a
situation that the layman recognizes as his own. Study that
begins with the revelatory literature of our time, such as
plays, novels, nonfiction documentaries, and cultural anal-
yses such as the works of Riesman, Whyte, and Mills,
mentioned above, provides an excellent prelude to the gospel. It encourages the layman to speak more freely about
his real feelings and questions. Theological insights may
then be discussed in the group in response to these questions and in dialogue with the real dynamics of modern life.

POLITICAL APATHY

The political attitude of the other-directed person is best
described as indifferentism, according to Riesman. Toler-
ance and passivity, rather than the moralizing posture often
taken by the inner-directed person, typify his reaction to
political questions. He feels controlled by the impersonal
workings of fate in the area of political decisions as well as
in his business and social life. He feels helpless in the face
of political developments, and steers clear of any direct exercise of political responsibility because of this dominant
attitude of fatalism. He is a spectator of the political scene,
feeling unable to influence in any significant way the course
of political events which determine so many aspects of his
life:

> Since popular culture is in essence a tutor of consump-
> tion, it teaches the other-directed man to consume poli-
> tics and to regard politics and political information and
> attitudes as consumption goods. They are products,
> games, entertainments, recreations; and he is their pur-
> chaser, player, spectator, or leisure-time observer.[49]

If the other-directed person is political at all, he is related to the political scene as a member of what Riesman calls a " veto group," by which he means any special interest group that has political influence. He leaves it to the veto group to defend his interests, co-operating with them when he is called upon to vote or to apply pressure through such means as petitions, letters, and telegrams.

Perhaps it is this political indifferentism and fatalism which accounts for the general failure, or the very limited success, of the social education and action programs of the few churches that even attempt them. In his book *The Christian Gospel and the Parish Church*, Charles D. Kean reminds us that our laymen live in the particular, in both a political and an economic sense. Their political and economic concerns are generally confined to the relation between political and economic factors and their own families, their neighborhoods, and their jobs.[50] They tend to be interested in politics only at points where they can perceive this relationship. They will often listen politely and passively to panels, lectures, and forums that deal in broad generalities concerning the Christian's responsibility in politics. But they will only become intimately and personally involved in the social education and action program of the church if it begins with the political and economic questions that directly impinge upon their occupations, their families, their homes and neighborhoods, and the special veto groups related to these. National and world events occasionally force them to place these concerns in a larger perspective; but usually they are less concerned with matters of high policy than they are with more immediate issues. The church must speak to them initially in terms of this narrower social world which has immediate reality for them.

The laymen's veto groups, such as their professional and

commercial associations, their taxpayers' associations, their PTA's, etc., are centered around these three areas of concern: family, neighborhood, and job — and their political interests start (and too often end) right there. The layman will only become deeply concerned over broader national and international issues as he is led to comprehend their relationship to more localized and personal concerns. Speaking of the layman as he sees him, Robert Lynn of the Montview Boulevard Presbyterian Church in Denver writes:

> His growing sense of alienation from the world (and therefore his flight into political apathy) is not overcome by asking him to study the latest and "best" guide to national and international social issues. He will not be able to act or respond until he understands himself.[51]

The question "Who am I?" in terms of specific social relationships, logically and psychologically precedes the question "What am I going to do about it?" in terms of Christian political responsibility.

Politically, the layman's identity, the answer to the question "Who am I?" is bound up with his relation to his particular veto groups. Only when he has been led to realize this is he ready to come to grips with the ethical question "What am I going to do about it?" We must face the fact that the layman rarely sees any relationship between the policies of the veto groups to which he belongs and the norms of Christian ethics. He is inclined to acknowledge the validity of these norms only as they apply to him as an individual or to his immediate family relationships. He pictures himself as a "moral man in immoral society" and lets it go at that. He needs to be guided toward a less individualistic conception of Christian ethics, and toward a realization of the far-reaching national and international impact of the actions of his veto groups. He must be brought to recognize the demand that the gospel places upon him to bear witness to it in the policy-making work of his veto groups, in order that Christ may indeed be the "transformer of culture," to use Richard Niebuhr's phrase.

The political indifferentism of our laymen, however, cannot very well be overcome by a frontal attack loaded with moralistic exhortations regarding the Christian duty toward responsible political participation. A better strategy for Christian adult education would seem to lie in dealing with political and economic problems as they are related to other problems under discussion in vocational groups, parents classes, neighborhood zone groups, and other types of groups in the parish. One of the major shortcomings of much of the denominational and interdenominational study material in the areas of Christian vocational responsibility and family life education is a failure to come to grips with the political and economic pressures and problems that directly impinge upon the layman's work and family life. This has unfortunate results both for the understanding of vocational and family life problems and for social education and action.

The political apathy of our laymen can be converted to active concern only when they are able to see the relationship of political and economic questions to other questions they are discussing in the light of the gospel. Furthermore, the laymen must see issues of immediate concern to them in a Christian perspective before they can see other broader issues in the same perspective. A discussion group centering around denominational social pronouncements would doubtless be very interesting in a general way, at least to a few people. But such pronouncements can be more fruitfully used as auxiliary resource material, reflecting the representative opinion of the churches and throwing light on other discussion topics more immediately related to our laymen's particular interests. In discussion groups that are concerned mainly with Bible study, these pronouncements can occasionally be used effectively to illustrate how Christians seek to relate Biblical affirmations to present social realities.

Denominational social pronouncements will seem important and relevant to most laymen only in terms of their Biblical context or as they are related to issues with which the laymen are in immediate touch. It is always " safe " to have discussions on " distant " issues; but growth in Christian social concern must begin with issues that call for a more personal ethical response than writing a letter to Washington. *Growth in Christian political responsibility moves from the particular to the general, as in all learning experiences.*

The minister must seek to overcome the abstraction of social education and action from the immediate interests of the laymen. Furthermore, as a responsible resource person in organizational program-planning, he must also seek to overcome its abstraction from the general programing in the adult organizations of the church. Social education and action ought to be an integral part of every aspect of the total adult program of the local church, if people are to be made aware of the corporate as well as the individual relevance of the Christian gospel. It should not be the separated and isolated activity and concern of a few " interested " persons, but a properly emphasized feature of the program of all the church's organizations. If we do allow social education and action to be confined to one small group of adults in the parish, we not only deny, in effect, that intelligent social witnessing is the responsibility of every member of the church, but we may also find that the group attracts many chronic malcontents and neurotic people who seek to vent their hostility under the benevolent disguise of Christian social action.

The Influence of the Mass Media

Closely related to the problems of other-directedness is the impact of the mass media upon the layman. Everett C. Parker and his associates, in their monumental study, *The Television-Radio Audience and Religion*, call attention to an unprecedented shift in people's attention from opinion-forming groups and agencies that are local and personal to those which are national and impersonal, the most important of these being radio and television. The New Haven survey conducted by Parker and his collaborators indicated that the clergy of New Haven were exposed to these mass media less than any other professional group. They were inclined to discount the influence of the mass media on their parishioners' lives, " and in general were ready to continue to minister as though these media did not exist." [52] The researchers conclude that Protestant ministers must be made aware of the powerful influence that the mass media have on their parishioners, and that one of the goals of Christian education in the churches should be to make the members of the church conscientious stewards in the use of the mass media in their homes.[53] Riesman too is quite aware of the degree to which laymen have their source of other-direction in the symbols and stereotypes of the mass media, particularly in the ordering of their family life.[54]

The problems posed by the phenomenal impact of mass communication seem to have three major implications for adult Christian education. First of all, one must agree with Everett Parker that it is the responsibility of the church to educate its laymen toward a conscientious stewardship in the use of the mass media. This will involve helping our laymen to develop sound psychological and theological bases for discrimination and criticism. Discussions in parents classes probably would be the most appropriate place for this, inasmuch as the impact of the mass media is most keenly felt in the area of family relations. Such discussions could be helpful to parents in developing standards for selecting the programs to which their children are to be exposed, and for making parents more consciously critical of the sub-Christian values that they themselves might otherwise absorb from the mass media. It is incumbent upon the minister to keep himself reasonably well informed (i.e., somewhat better informed than the average minister in the New Haven survey!) concerning the religious and secular ideas communicated to the laymen through the mass media, if he is to aid them in the process of evaluation.

Secondly, the minister must take into account the fact that the mass media tend to condition his laymen to expect predigested religious information from the church, just as the mass media give them predigested information on everything else from the news of the day to scientific developments. Therefore, when a study group is started it may be wise to use some of the highly simplified primers for laymen which have recently appeared on the market in great numbers, such as the excellent little books in the Layman's Theological Library series. A group may decide later that it is ready to wrestle with more basic material. One of the best features of the adult education curriculum provided for discussion groups by the Great Books Foundation is that from year to year there is in the series a very gradual progression in the difficulty of the content. This would also be a sound procedure for study groups in the church. Adults whose general reading is at no more profound a level than *The Reader's Digest* cannot be expected to gravitate immediately to the writings of the best contemporary theologians. After all, the apostle Paul himself first fed his Corinthian brethren with the milk of the gospel before giving them its solid meat!

Finally, the adult education program of the church should provide for the give-and-take of *two*-way communication within the dynamics of small groups. We live in an age when the adult is increasingly subjected to only one-way communication, as the mass media encroach more and more upon his waking hours. In their emptiness, loneliness, and isolation, many people are psychologically and spiritually starving for want of two-way communication with other persons. This is one of the reasons professional counselors of all types are in such demand. In a social world where there is so little two-way communication, many people can find sympathetic and understanding listeners only by paying for them. A small study group under democratic leadership can provide the kind of two-way communication that not only requires the layman to think more deeply than the mass media usually make him, but which also counteracts the dehumanizing encroachments of the mass media's one-way communication into his leisure time. The layman can stay home any night of the week and be talked to by panels and forums and lectures on television. The group life of the church must offer him something more than this if it is to attract him.

THE BREAKDOWN OF COMMUNITY

One of the most prominent developments in American society is the gradual breakdown of genuine community through the processes of urbanization. Although urban life is massively organized in terms of specialized functions, it is actually dispersive in its effect upon close human relations. Anonymous or essentially commercial contacts characterize many if not most of the associations people have with one another. There has been a marked decline in the strength of social bonds in all phases of urban life. The problem is created in part by the great social and geographical mobility of our people. The " displaced persons " of our time are not only those who have been uprooted by wars and revolutions. They are also those who have been uprooted geographically and socially by participation in victory, by their success and advancement in the great impersonal processes of production and distribution.

Nor does this general breakdown of community seem to be arrested by the " flight to the suburbs." Social anonymity seems to be as great or even greater in the suburbs, especially in those newer and smaller suburbs which do not have the extensive recreational, social, and commercial facilities that in urban areas serve as centers for community life. The residents of suburbia, more of whom are on the middle and upper rungs of the success ladder than their city brethren, are even more afflicted with the problems of social and geographical mobility. The fact that the great corporations for which many of them work often transfer them quite suddenly from place to place poses a great problem.

This high population mobility has had a particularly devastating effect on that most basic community of all, the family. The fact that very often no more than two generations live under the same roof, or even in the same general geographical area, means that many young parents are deprived of the normative child-raising guidance which was, in a bygone era, traditionally given by grandparents and other close relatives. Riesman points out that parents, increasingly in doubt as to how to bring up their children, are turning to their contemporaries and the mass media rather than to the older generation for advice. The churches must take this need for child-raising guidance into consideration in planning their programs of Christian family life education. Since, in any event, our rather other-directed parents are taking their cues for the ordering of family life from their contemporaries, let us provide for this in a Christian setting. Small discussion groups composed of parents who are seeking to relate their faith to their family life, and whose children are in approximately the same age range, provide just such a setting. In small groups of parents it is possible to attain varying degrees of consensus which would help to counteract the prevailing normlessness and confusion that has resulted from the geographical " segregation of the generations."

The great proliferation of voluntary associations and special interest groups of all kinds that has accompanied the gradual increase of leisure time in our society is not in itself a countervailing tendency toward the restoration of true community. The true community cannot be simply defined as an area of interest common to a number of people in association with one another. Professional organizations, service clubs, and other special interest groups are properly called associations, not communities. As Baker Brownell points out in his book *The Human Community*, true community exists only where the area of common interest includes each individual in his entirety.[55]

The adult education movement in the church today will not contribute to the restoration of community simply by adding educational programs and study groups to the parish organization. There can be no recovery of genuine Christian community in the church through the multiplication of special interest groups that are almost exclusively content-centered. The mere sharing of religious information and opinion can only result in an impersonal, abstracted, and partial relationship among people. Small study groups can aid the layman's quest for community only in so far as techniques are utilized that foster genuine encounter between persons as well as with the subject matter so that there is a real sharing of self with self as whole persons.

THE ALIEN WORLD OF THEOLOGY AND THE BIBLE

It is somewhat perilous to make sweeping generalizations concerning the religious faith, knowledge, and attitudes of the layman. The average church usually contains parishioners of widely varying degrees of theological sophistication and spiritual maturity. Nevertheless, there is some validity in this line of approach once we have acknowledged that almost every church has members who cannot be included in any general statement concerning " the average layman."

One of the most perceptive evaluations of lay religion written in recent years is Canon Wedel's book *The Christianity of Main Street*. Wedel observes that the " Christianity of Main Street " in America is in danger of becoming a vague faith in ethical principles and values that have no Biblical or theological rootage, an illiterate Christianity living under the illusion that such illiteracy does not matter very much. The very word "theology" has become largely suspect and is regarded as the province of "the theologians " and as strictly " off limits " for laymen. The secularized Christianity of Main Street is essentially a humanistic faith, a system of ethical ideals lacking organic relation to the Christian doctrines from which they originally arose.[56] Similarly Will Herberg, in his book *Protestant-Catholic-Jew*, declares that America's high ethical idealism, its " common faith," has been divorced from its historical rootage in the Judaeo-Christian tradition.[57] The conviction is prevalent among our laymen that religion is in essence an ethical opinion, that religion and ethics are virtually identical. The essential thing is morality, and religion is a useful means of achieving this end.

One of the most lamentable results of this separation of ethics from theology is the undermining of parental authority concerning standards of conduct. It is natural for children to react negatively and rebelliously toward standards of behavior that have no apparent basis other than the will of the parents. Parental moralism that lacks any transcendent sanction, any relationship to Christian convictions, has no real authority for the child, beyond the fear of punishment or the hope of reward. The moral authority that parents possess can only be strengthened when parents themselves are able to articulate the relationship between their Christian beliefs and the behavioral requirements they set for their children. This can best be achieved when the program of adult Christian education integrates theologically grounded ethics into the content of the adult curriculum, especially in parents classes. However, the way in which theology as such is dealt with in study groups must be carefully thought out. Although local situations will differ, the lack of interest that so often characterizes the initial reactions of our laymen in regard to theology would seem to indicate that very often Christian doctrine had best be approached *indirectly* through its relation to Biblical studies and ethical problems and other areas where the layman's more immediate interests lie, rather than in abstraction from them. Laymen frequently show an interest in Biblical theology, whereas they are often quite uninterested in the more strictly philosophical types of theology.

Closely related to the layman's indifference to theology as such is his alienation from the thought world of the Bible. This does not mean that the layman is *uninterested* in the Bible. It merely means that he is unable to comprehend most of it, and therefore shows little interest in reading it by himself. He has a vague attitude of reverence toward the Bible, but he has a feeling of helplessness with regard to it because he doesn't know how to read it. Hendrik Kraemer is acutely aware of this problem of communication between the Bible and the modern layman, and states it quite clearly:

> We must recognize the unintelligibility of the Bible, not only of its language, its terminology, but also, to use a German word, of its *Weltbild* (picture of the world). This affects people as antiquated, archaic, unscientific. . . . It sounds so strange, so incomprehensible, so distant from their ordinary ways of thinking. It is, at best, to them a " sacral " language, as all sacral languages wrapped up in mystery. It is, they think, a book for experts and theologians. . . . The decisive point in connection with the breakdown of communication is the dominant trend in the modern apperception of the totality of life, which seems to be worlds apart from the Biblical apperception. The last is Chinese to the ordinary man. There is an incompatibility of languages to the extent, it seems, of mutual intranslatability. It seems an insoluble dilemma.[58]

We may not share Kraemer's pessimism concerning a solution, but it would be difficult to contradict his statement of the problem. The modern layman sees little direct relation between his thought patterns and his ways of reacting to things and the concerns of the Bible. He and the Bible simply do not share the same universe of discourse. They do not speak the same language.

This " confusion of tongues," which hinders and obstructs the dialogue between modern man and the Bible, must be taken into account by any philosophy of adult Christian education that would stress Biblical content in the curriculum. There are two methods for tackling this problem: either we must make the Bible come to terms with the secular world view of our laymen, or our laymen must be brought to terms with the world view of the Bible. If we choose the former alternative, our curriculum will be concerned with study *about* the Bible rather than with Bible study. We shall avoid using Biblical language and symbolism wherever possible. We shall present the Word only after we have " demythologized " it. We shall present theology, even Biblical theology, as a substitute for the encounter with the Bible itself, and only after we have substituted contemporary symbols for the Biblical ones. But in this event, our teaching ministry will be, not a service of the Word, but a service of words about the Word. Our laymen will be given only the Biblical content that we preselect and predigest and spoon-feed to them. They will not be equipped by this method to read the Bible for themselves. They will remain dependent upon us for their understanding of its message.

The latter and preferable alternative — bringing the layman to terms with the world view of the Bible — will necessitate educating our laymen to understand Biblical myth and symbolism so that they themselves may enter what Karl Barth calls " the strange new world of the Bible " and thus encounter the Book itself, and not simply our reviews and condensations of it. If we decide to lead our laymen into a closer acquaintance with the world view of the Bible, our task will be one of *re*mythologizing the Bible, instead of " *de*mythologizing " it as Rudolf Bultmann and his disciples would advocate. This is essentially a task of translation, of redefinition and restatement, whereby the layman may be enabled to see the validity of Biblical myth and symbol as a means of conveying truths that apply to his situation but that cannot be contained in simple propositions.

We must realize, of course, that both the formal training and the experience of most of our laymen incline them to interpret all verbal information in a very literal sense. They have difficulty grasping poetic and metaphorical meanings such as are conveyed by Biblical myth and symbol. But their literal-mindedness must be challenged at this point, if we are to help them avoid either the extreme of rigid fundamentalism or the other extreme of rejecting the Biblical message because it seems unscientific or irrelevant to their situation. An example of the semantic difficulties we may expect in group discussions with these literal-minded laymen of ours is given in the experience reported by Thomas M. Steen, co-minister of the Asbury-First Methodist Church in Rochester, New York. Commenting on his adult education work there, Steen writes:

> We soon ran into one of our major problems, one which we have experienced since then in every one of our groups: clarifying our understanding of religious words and symbols. A vocabulary can be a means of separating people as well as of uniting them. We often spent a whole evening attempting to arrive at an understanding of a word or phrase. . . . This experience itself indicates how inadequate it is simply to preach the Word from the pulpit. The church must find a way whereby words can grow new meanings and make communication possible.[59]

It would be difficult to overemphasize the problems involved in establishing communication between our laymen and the language and ideas of the Bible. But Steen's testimony, and that of others, indicates that such semantic struggles in discussion groups are well worth the effort in leading laymen to the point where they are Biblically literate without being Biblical literalists.

Without an interpretation of Biblical myth and symbolism that will enable laymen to take it *seriously* if not literally, the abyss between them and the Bible will remain as insurmountable as Hendrik Kraemer pictures it to be. Unless we increase their acquaintance with Biblical symbols, large sections of the Bible will remain unknown territory for the great majority, and an unhealthy refuge for others. The present " confusion of tongues " between our laymen and the Bible underlines the inanity of the pious and moralistic exhortations to read the Bible which many pastors direct toward their people. They cannot read it with understanding unless they understand its symbolism, and unless they have been helped to relate the enduring meanings behind the Biblical myths and symbols to their present condition.

The minister must admit his share of the blame for the present situation of the layman with regard to the Bible. The layman's alienation from the thought world of the Bible, and his " implicit fundamentalism," as Randolph C. Miller has called it, which actually contributes to this alienation, can largely be laid to the failure of the minister as preacher and as teacher to interpret Biblical symbolism, and his failure to introduce the findings of modern Biblical scholarship where they are needed for Biblical interpretation. Earl F. Zeigler asserts that the church has felt compelled through the centuries to deny to its laity much information which only the clergy dared have. The situation, he declares, is reminiscent of ancient Judaism, where only the high priest ever entered the Holy of Holies, and the sacred law could be handled only by people selected for that purpose.[60]

Since the evidence on many points of Biblical criticism is admittedly not absolutely conclusive, or since the minister supposes that his people are not ready to absorb the shock of becoming acquainted with highly probable hypotheses which he himself knows, the minister often will not take his people into his confidence and will withhold scholarly findings which crucially influence Biblical interpretation. But when he does this he places the Bible in a false light. He exposes those whom he teaches to the later conclusion that their minister is either ignorant or deceitful; and he has to make peace with his conscience for having entered into a conspiracy for the suppression of knowledge.

Protestantism has traditionally stressed the importance of placing the Bible in the hands of the laity; yet Protestant ministers often withhold those well-established critical findings which they regard as essential to their own understanding of the Bible but which, paradoxically, they consider unessential for the layman's understanding of it. As Randolph C. Miller says in his book *Biblical Theology and Christian Education:*

> There is a great gap . . . between what the Biblical scholars believe and teach and what the layman and the church school teachers know about the Bible. This may be discovered in almost all lesson materials for church schools. It is almost as if all the discoveries of more than a century are the private property of the scholars. . . . The intelligent layman who is proud of his knowledge of the Bible often believes that Moses wrote the Pentateuch or that there is no difference in the historical value of the Synoptic Gospels and the Fourth Gospel. Some of this ignorance is due to an unwritten conspiracy of silence on the part of the clergy, who should know better but who are afraid or find it expedient not to upset the settled beliefs of their congregations.[61]

There is danger, of course, that the minister will be tempted to play only the part of the iconoclast, shattering long-held assumptions chiefly for shock effect and failing to fill this void with the more positive conceptions of the nature of Biblical revelation which modern criticism provides. But if he is convinced that certain findings of Biblical criticism are essential to his own apprehension of the Biblical drama, then the withholding of this information from the laity is not only intellectual dishonesty but a failure to discharge adequately his teaching ministry to his laymen, no matter how much Bible study he may give them nor how " Biblical " his sermons may be.

However, there are limitations to preaching as a vehicle for equipping the layman with the critical tools necessary for reading the Bible intelligently. A sermon is not a seminary lecture, and therefore it is better suited for the interpretation of Biblical key words and symbols than it is for the presentation of critical findings. In a sermon the latter may only shock and disturb people, since there is not time enough for an adequate presentation of evidence and no provision at all for the discussion of the questions the people would inevitably want to ask. Therefore, it would seem that the disclosure of such important but potentially upsetting information is best achieved within small study groups, which can provide suitable opportunities for further questions and elucidations.

Nor is it enough that the layman be provided with only the general outlines of Biblical criticism. He also needs specific " footnotes," either verbal or written, to the passages of the Bible that he is studying. These may be provided orally in study groups where the minister or a well-prepared layman functions as a resource person on such matters, and in written form by furnishing the layman with annotated Bible texts. Particularly useful are the inexpensive paper-bound books of the Bible in Harper & Brothers Annotated Bible Series, and William Barclay's The Daily Study Bible series on the books of the New Testament. And certainly a set of *The Interpreter's Bible* together with the *Westminster Study Edition of The Holy Bible* and the *Abingdon Bible Commentary* are " musts " for every church library as resources which our laymen are quite capable of using to prepare themselves for study group leadership and participation. Unless we provide our laymen with resources such as these, we have no just reason to be dismayed if they turn up with inadequate or fundamentalist resource tools they have come across in local bookstores or in the Standard Press and David C. Cook catalogues.

The Roman Catholic Church has been far ahead of us in providing its laymen with annotated Bible texts. Its authorized Douay Version, which is widely used, supplies just such notations along with the approved translation. There is the danger, of course, that the Protestant layman may take as uncritical and credulous an attitude toward the notations in his material as the Roman Catholic takes toward the Douay footnotes; but if material is used that presents variant interpretations, and if the minister makes clear the contingent nature of all such comments on the text, this danger can be avoided.

CHAPTER FIVE

The Layman: Tomorrow

WE HAVE examined some of the salient characteristics of the layman in contemporary middle-class society and some of the chief problems that presently confront him: great manipulative pressures toward conformity, the impact of the mass media, political apathy, the breakdown of true community, ethical humanism, and alienation from the Bible. This has given us in brief outline the " present picture " of our laymen. But underneath these contemporary problems run the undercurrents of man's enduring predicaments as man — the " perennial picture," so to speak. These interact with the more strictly contemporary problems of our laymen, both as cause and as effect or symptom, and perhaps they should be considered as being of even greater importance in forming a philosophy and strategy of adult Christian education. H. Richard Niebuhr rightly warns us that: " We can make far too much of the changing needs of men in changing civilizations. Religion is a highly conservative thing because the fundamental needs of men as finite and delinquent creatures aspiring after infinity and wholeness do not change." [62]

AGE GROUP PROBLEMS

In addition to an appraisal of the general social, intellectual, and cultural situation of our laymen and its implications for adult education, it is important to take some cognizance of the specific problems usually associated with the various age levels of adulthood. We simply cannot ignore the very real differences between young adulthood, the middle years, and old age as to the central needs and crises that usually attend each of these stages.

We must remind ourselves of the fact that the young adult years normally constitute a " settling-down " period, a time for making basic identifications and decisions in areas such as vocation, marriage, and religion. Young adults are in a stage of transition from circumscribed, sheltered, and dependent modes of living into a world of vocational and marital responsibility. Everett Parker and his associates conducted a survey of homes in the greater New Haven area, which indicated that, as one would expect, the couples under forty years of age were primarily preoccupied with interests centering around their families, their homes, and their social status.[63] The prime attention given to the problems of marriage and the family at this age may serve as an excellent point of contact between the church and these younger adults. Many of them who seem to be uninterested in the traditional type of adult Bible class would more likely be attracted to parents discussion groups. Starting from this basic focus of interest, it is then possible to branch out into related areas of concern which bear upon the problems they face. Bible study, social education and action, vocational issues, Christian doctrine, and other subject matter will enlist the interest of young men and women who have grasped the relation between these areas of concern and the problems of marriage and parenthood.

The basic problem of the middle years of adulthood, according to Lewis J. Sherrill, is the problem of meaning, the task of achieving a mature view of life and of one's place in it.[64] He is supported in this contention by Carl Jung, who writes in his *Modern Man in Search of a Soul:*

> Among my patients in the second half of life — that is to say, over thirty-five — there has not been one whose problem in the last resort was not that of finding a religious outlook on life. It is safe to say that every one of them feel ill because he has lost that which the living religions of every age have given their followers, and none of them has been really healed who did not regain his religious outlook.[65]

We often accuse the average middle-class, middle-aged congregation of being anti-intellectual; but there is, ironically enough, an anti-intellectualism implicit in our assumption that their apparent indifference to theology truly represents their most deeply personal attitudes toward life. We cannot ignore the deeply religious questions of these people simply because they may not yet have reached the point where they are able to give them conscious formulation.

Robert Lynn believes that these middle years provide the most valid and promising focus of attention for Christian education. On the basis of his experience he declares that:

> A growing number of churchgoers want to be *literate* Christians for whom faith in God is a means of understanding their world and themselves. This assertion might seem unbelievable to those who encounter daily the apparently self-inflicted theological illiteracy of so many Protestants. But, if our experience in Montview Church means anything, a surprisingly large minority of Protestants are not satisfied with their intellectual *status quo*. They want to develop an interpretation of life that is both intellectually honest and seriously Christian.[66]

It is during these middle years of life (thirty to sixty) that the search for ultimate meaning is most intense. During these years the ultimate questions are raised, consciously or unconsciously, as children are born and reared and family responsibilities become more pressing, and as these adults face sickness and the approaching end of their earthly existence. Many men in the ministry, particularly younger men, who are somewhat dissatisfied with the parish ministry and who have been toying for years with the idea of " going into teaching " can find within this numerically predominant age group excellent God-given opportunities for " going into teaching " right in their present parishes! There is no reason at all why the local church cannot carry on an educational program as intellectually stimulating as that provided on the college campuses, especially when we take into consideration the greater maturity and wealth of experience that these adults in their middle years possess.

The advancing years bring with them a host of new problems; but perhaps the one most difficult for older adults is the problem of loneliness. Their search for community does not cease with the passing of the years, but rather becomes the more urgent. Bereavement separates them from their mates, retirement separates them from their fellow workers, and distance often separates them from their children and grandchildren. Their problem of loneliness, their need to feel needed, can be met effectively in the fellowship of small study groups in the church which accept them, give meaningful content to their leisure hours, and stimulate them mentally.

The main value, however, of an understanding of the problems more or less peculiar to the various adult age levels would seem to lie in the area of one's personal pastoral ministry to individuals, except in so far as it is possible for the leader of a study group to personalize the direction of the discussion in terms of the age levels represented in the group. For years now, leaders in many churches have thought that ideally their adult education program should segregate people quite distinctly in accordance with age differences. Religious educators have long assumed that the pattern of physical and psychological growth provides a useful framework for ordering the educational program of the church. However, we must recognize that although there obviously are definite stages in man's physical and psychological development, these stages are not automatically and at the same time stages of spiritual development, in terms of his relation to God.

It is misleading to overemphasize the distinctness with which the problem of making basic life decisions, the problem of searching for ultimate meaning, and the problem of loneliness are related to particular adult age groups. To a degree, these problems are common to all adults. Adults of all ages have much to contribute to one another through the sharing of experiences and insights within the context of group study. Thus, there is much to be gained in organizing the group life of the church in such a way that the various age groups will not be too strictly segregated. Church family night programs and the rotation plan for women's circles are corrective steps in this direction.

Many ministers who are doing some of the most creative work with small study groups in their churches report that neither they nor the groups themselves have desired any deliberate age stratification — not even in quite large churches where such segregation of age groupings might be more easily achieved. What is probably even more significant is the fact that the laymen themselves have not tended toward any such stratification in the pattern of their voluntary affiliations with these groups.

Ministers are trained to think of people as young adults, or adults in their middle years, or adults in their "years of fulfillment." The current jargon provides many synonyms for these three age categories. They are certainly useful as analytic terms in the discussion of religious education theory; but many successful ventures in the field of adult education through small groups provide us with impressive evidence that, on the whole, adults neither desire nor need to be segregated along these three basic age lines (with the obvious exception of *unmarried* young adults, who usually desire separate grouping to some extent). For every elderly person who would be interested in a " Golden Age Club " in the church, there are usually several others who would avoid identification with such a group as they would avoid being committed to a home for the aged. If there is no such club in the community, it might be very much in order for the church to minister to the social and recreational needs of older adults in this way. But if we are correct in identifying loneliness as a major problem of old age, the church will be ministering more effectively to its older adults if its educational program provides them with channels of association and communication that include a wider circle of adults than the rocking-chair brigade.

Speaking of the older adults in one of the study groups in his church which grew out of his Lenten neighborhood groups, Gerald Jud declares:

> One of the most important and exciting aspects of this group is the very warmhearted response it has made to ten quite elderly people. Although there are some very young couples in the group, and the majority are below fifty, it has given a place of real significance to these older people. I believe that older people ought not to be segregated in the church but ought to be integral parts of the group life that cuts across many age divisions. And in this

group the point is illustrated that older people may be related to the church in a most intimate way; they are able to contribute to the discussion the wisdom of the years, and they rejoice in the wonderful feeling of being accepted by the other members of the group.[67]

In our teaching ministry to individuals of different ages in our study groups we must remain aware of the particular problems and needs that are more or less characteristic of the various stages of adulthood, just as Paul was aware of the important differences between Jewish and Gentile Christians, between men and women, between slaves and freemen in his churches. He expressed his pastoral concern by devoting considerable attention to these differences in his letters. But as he himself says: " In Christ Jesus you are all sons of God, through faith. . . . There is neither Jew nor Greek, there is neither slave nor free, there is neither male nor female; for you are all one in Christ Jesus." (Gal. 3:26, 28.) So also, " in Christ," as men and women before God, in the redemptive community which itself stands in constant need of redemption, the enduring predicaments of human life provide a common focus for adult education compared to which all age group considerations are quite secondary.

THE ENDURING PREDICAMENTS

Probably one of the most pervasive predicaments of modern man is a sense of estrangement — from self, from God, and from his fellows. Contemporary symptoms of this are the loneliness and homelessness of the layman amidst the high mobility and urbanization of society, which we discussed in the previous chapter as the superficial social relatedness of the " other-directed " and the breakdown of true community. Concerning a Personal Issues Inventory which he administered to 229 graduate students at Teachers College, Columbia University, Arthur T. Jersild reported that almost half of his respondents identified one or more conditions of loneliness as representing a problem in their lives with which they felt they needed help. Some of the most gripping expressions of their loneliness were voiced as feelings of homelessness. Over one third of those who were tested by this Personal Issues Inventory identified one or more conditions of homelessness as a personal issue they needed help in facing.[68] These graduate students represented a very wide range of social backgrounds and ages; and probably many of those who did not indicate estrangement and loneliness as a personal issue face this predicament but are unable or unwilling to verbalize it.

In his book *Anxiety in Christian Experience*, Wayne E. Oates points out that loneliness is the central quality that characterizes every major type of anxiety. Economic anxiety tends to isolate men from one another through the pressures of competition. Anxiety over the finitude of one's life and over limitations in one's abilities and accomplishments has the same effect. The anxiety of grief is essentially a lonely, incommunicable experience, as is also the anxiety of guilt. And the person suffering from the anxiety of legalism feels that he must earn his own salvation, apart from the grace of both human and divine fellowship.[69] To a greater or lesser extent all these anxieties are experienced in every human life; and in every case the anxiety has some rootage in man's loneliness, his partial estrangement from self, from God, and from other persons.

In addition to helping to create anxiety feelings, this threefold condition of estrangement contributes to the feeling that life is devoid of enduring meaning. As Martin Buber has suggested, a sense of life's meaningfulness is dependent upon personal relationships among men and between man and God; and the breakdown of these relationships thus results in a loss of a sense of meaning. Indeed, we might even speak of human despair over the intrinsic meaningfulness of human life as yet another type or category of anxiety. Paul Tillich believes that the "anxiety of meaninglessness and fate" is the central category of anxiety in the modern era.[70] Life seems to lack ultimate purpose and direction. Modern man feels that he is in the clutches of vast impersonal forces which alone control his destiny.

The political indifferentism of the middle-class masses seems to be but one symptom of this fatalism. Man regards himself as a pawn in the hands of vast economic forces, the inner circles of national and international politics, and the iron laws of nature and technology. God, however potentially powerful, seems very far off. "The cry for salvation that such men make," says H. Richard Niebuhr, "is the cry for freedom from the 'other-directedness' and heteronomy of existence, from the life of mass man."[71] Tillich writes, "It is not an exaggeration to say that today man experiences his present situation in terms of disruption, conflict, self-destruction, meaninglessness, and despair in all realms of life." The answer to this situation, he feels, is "a reality in which the self-estrangement of our existence is overcome, a reality of reconciliation and reunion, of creativity, meaning, and hope."[72] The church can be such a reality when it simultaneously provides Christian fellowship and Christian learning, the experience of reconciliation together with the experience of mental creativity, meaning, and hope.

The search for salvation is at once a quest for wholeness, for a restoration of broken relationships with God and other men, and for a recovery of ultimate meaning. Because man's doubt and despair are interrelated with his condition of estrangement, and because the discovery of ultimate meaning takes place within the context of personal relationships, the adult educator must seek to help laymen simultaneously in their search for meaning and in their quest for community. The task of adult education is not merely the imparting of religious knowledge; it is also the work of building Christian community within which both verbal language and the language of relationships mutually reinforce each other in communicating the gospel of reconciliation and hope to man in his estrangement and despair. In the following chapters we will trace the outline of a small-group approach to adult education on the part of the church and its ministry which may effectively mediate God's answer to man's deepest needs.

CHAPTER SIX:

Divine Revelation Through Study Groups

FROM what was said in the first section concerning the nature of the church and its ministry as servants of the Word of God, it follows that we may define the minister's primary task as communicating the gospel to his laymen and utilizing every means at his disposal to help the church become a community within which and through which God reveals himself. The assumption upon which the following treatment of the church's task in adult education is based is that the answer to the layman's profoundest needs lies in God's self-revelation. A further assumption is made, namely, that God's revelation does not answer man's needs simply by increasing his religious knowledge, but by bringing about a reconciliation that restores the broken relationships between man and himself, his God, and his fellows. Revelation occurs within the context of a community of Christians *in* their interaction with one another and *within* the encompassing presence of the Holy Spirit. The ultimate criterion for the ordering of the relationships among the laymen in the church and between the laymen and the minister is the facilitation of this dynamic process of continuing revelation.

In the third chapter we examined some of the ways in which doctrinal and expository preaching, the reading of the Word, and the enacted Word in Baptism and the Lord's

Supper could be utilized to fulfill the teaching function of the ministry. However, we also noted that these channels of communication essentially involve the entire congregation. Their importance for adult Christian education certainly deserves fuller recognition than has been given in recent years. But we also noted that these channels have many limitations, and that educational work in small groups is essential for an adequate program of adult Christian education. In this chapter we will explore more fully the unique potentialities of small groups for adult education.

The whole history of revelation, the whole story of God's dealings with man, is a record of his working with the individual *in community*. The creative interaction that often occurs within small groups of Christians, struggling together to hear what God has spoken through his Word and what he continues to say to them in the events of the day and in their personal experiences, constitutes an important medium through which he continues to confront them. The testimony of centuries of Christian experience is that small groups have often been the vehicles of revelation in ways that entire churches have not.

Repeatedly throughout history the church has been regenerated and renewed as God has used small, intimate groups of concerned Christians as a means of recovering the original vitality of Biblical revelation and as media through which his Word has brought forth new revelation. The *ecclesiola in ecclesia*, the "church within the church," has often been the source and stimulus for the continuing reformation of the church toward closer accordance with the Word of God.

Ministers who say, "But we haven't time for this," or "We cannot justify spending such a disproportionate amount of time with so few of our people," should take a closer look at the history of the church. The church began with a small group of disciples. During the Middle Ages, it was partially reformed from within by the small groups of followers who gathered around such men as Benedict and St. Francis. In modern times, the Evangelical Revival in eighteenth-century England had as its starting point a group of four students at Oxford University, one of whom was John Wesley. The small " class meetings " inaugurated by Wesley were patterned after this Oxford group, and they were the vital center of the Methodist movement. In more recent years, the vitality of the new inner-city churches, such as the East Harlem Protestant Parish in New York City, has been largely attributable to their " group ministries " and neighborhood " agape " fellowships of prayer and study. The special potentiality of small study groups as effective channels of revelation and reconciliation is well summed up in this testimony of Harold R. Fray, Jr., minister of the Plymouth Congregational Church in Utica, New York:

> The development of small groups in the life of the church is not a gimmick. It is not a technique to add more pro-grams to churches, which, for the most part, are already overburdened with programs. The only purpose is to provide God with an effective channel of communica-tion, whereby he can reveal himself to his people and the gospel can become a living reality. Small groups, if they are to have a place in the life of our church, must be re-demptive fellowships of love in which the living Christ can be known. God alone can give birth to such a com-munity.[73]

Therapeutic Implications of Revelation

In the first section of this book, passing reference was made to the psychologically therapeutic potentialities of small study groups. At first glance, it may seem a bit strange to speak in this way of adult education in small groups. But if the assumption is true that God's self-revelation is his means of answering human needs, including psychological needs, then the revelatory processes of Christian education through which the Word of God is communicated are truly therapeutic in the deepest sense. Christian education at its best is a contemporary re-enactment of Biblical revelation; and therefore at its best it is likewise a " therapy of the soul," a healing of the whole man. Keeping in mind the threefold human predicament of estrangement from self, from God, and from one's fellow man mentioned in the last chapter, Lewis J. Sherrill's excellent definition of Christian education clearly indicates its therapeutic implications. " Christian education," he writes, " is the attempt, ordinarily by members of the Christian community, to participate in and to guide the changes which take place in persons in their relationship with God, with the church, with other persons, with the physical world, and with oneself." [74] As Christian education seeks to guide persons toward reconciliation in all these relationships, it serves the therapeutic function of aiding in the work of overcoming estrangement. The etymological relationship between the words " wholeness," " health," and " salvation " points to the profound relationship between the psychological concept of personal and interpersonal integration and the theological concept of redemption. In this sense, the words " therapeutic " and " redemptive " are virtually synonymous.

The words " Christian education," " reconciliation," " therapy," and " redemption " thus all point to realities that are very closely related. For everyone, reconciliation to God and to one's fellow man is essential to redemption, for it is primarily in and through these relationships that man needs to be redeemed. Especially in the case of disturbed, compulsive, unhappy people, the theological experience of reconciliation and redemption includes, in some degree, the psychological experience of reintegration. Experience shows that very anxious and even neurotic people who are in search of some saving help, which they are often unable to define, are particularly attracted to small study groups in the church. For all such people, the therapeutic potentialities inherent in these group experiences are particularly important. They can derive from them great psychological as well as spiritual benefit.

However, this aspect of group life should not tempt the adult educator to regard himself as a psychotherapist. He is no more equipped to resolve serious, deep-seated neuroses in a group situation than he is in the individual counseling situation. At best, his efforts will be ineffective with such people; at worst, he may do them considerable harm. Group therapy as such is a highly technical psychotherapeutic tool which can resolve psychological problems of serious depth only when employed by a skilled specialist. This does not mean that experiences in small study groups cannot have therapeutic results even though the leader is not a trained therapist, but only that such results should be a by-product, and not the deliberate and central aim, of the leader's efforts. Group therapy far exceeds the limitations of ordinary groups in the church in the *psychological* depth of the insights concerning oneself and one's relations with other people which it can bring. But at the same time, it must be said that a study group in the church can exceed the limitations of group therapy in its *theological* depth; for its therapeutic implications are not confined to the problems of human relations, but include also the divine-human relation.

This close relation between education and redemption, between therapy and reconciliation, is most clearly and effectively established in small study groups where the *gos-*

pel and the *fact* of reconciliation are both *heard* and *experienced* together. It is in groups of limited size, in which personal contacts are direct and informal, that men and women can best learn the meaning of their dependence on one another. However little they may initially be interested in any formal theory or doctrine concerning their interdependence, they become aware of it through their participation and sharing which develop latent creative forces within them. In this experience of interdependence and acceptance, reconciliation becomes a reality.

The language employed in current discussions on the nature of the church includes very frequent use of the technical New Testament term *koinōnia*. The term connotes a profound sharing, an intense belonging, within an intimate fellowship of Christians. It is often indiscriminately applied to the particular church as a whole, or even to a denomination or the church universal. But is *koinōnia*, in the New Testament sense of close and deep personal involvement with others, realizable in large groups? Beyond the little group where genuine human " belonging " is still possible, all talk of *koinōnia* becomes largely a matter of verbal pretense. Terms like " the church universal " or " the worldwide fellowship of the church " also become rather meaningless without this condition. It would seem that unless and until *koinōnia* is first experienced in small face-to-face groups it will remain a theological abstraction devoid of personal significance.

The language of personal relationships in small groups can reinforce and personalize the Christian message of reconciliation, and the reality of Christian *koinōnia*, which lonely and anxious men and women are eager to hear and to appropriate. The churches are full of lonely, estranged people who, though they may use the symbols and ceremonies of Christian reconciliation, have not actually experienced a relationship of trust and reconciliation with themselves, or with God, or with their fellow Christians. Yet such trust can be awakened, and this reconciliation experienced, through the dependable satisfaction of their psychological and spiritual needs within the interpersonal relationships of small groups. In this way, the religious language of reconciliation may become for them a saving reality.

The prime task of the church as the servant of the Word is to communicate the promise and the reality of reconciliation and redemption, which is the very heart of the Word. Indeed, it can be said that reconciliation to self, to man, and to God is *the* business of the church. Sometimes it is said that securing " commitment to Christ " is the prime task and main business of the church, and therefore the central goal of Christian education. But this seems to put things in the wrong order. It would be more accurate to say that the experience of *reconciliation* is *prior* to the decision of commitment; our commitment *follows* from this experience as our grateful response to God's reconciling activity in which he accepts us and overcomes our self-imposed estrangement from him. We are committed to Christ *because* God has reconciled us to himself through Christ. Any statement that the church's main purpose in Christian education is the " securing of commitment to Christ " is vulnerable to the charge of moralism or even of Pelagianism, since only the *prior* experience of *reconciliation* validates Christian commitment as a response to God's reconciling *grace,* a matter of " faith " rather than of " works."

As the new divine-human community created by God's Spirit, the church is set in the world to mediate the gift of God's reconciliation to man in his alienation and estrangement. This reconciling purpose provides a criterion for all the activities of the church. As George F. MacLeod, of the Church of Scotland's Iona Community, has aptly put it,

" The serious weekday business of a congregation is to create the apparatus for the exercise of reconciliation: reconciliation to each other because God has reconciled us to himself in Jesus Christ." [75] Surely many of the superficial and irrelevant concerns and activities in contemporary church life are attributable to the absence of an effective criterion for evaluating and judging all that the church is and does. Reconciliation is a key concept for understanding the purpose of the church, and as such it provides an excellent criterion for the ordering of parish life. The church as the body of Christ is a community within whose personal relationships the divine pledge of redemption through reconciliation is meant to be realized. We cannot even speak intelligently of redemption and reconciliation apart from these relationships.

Judged by the criterion of what best facilitates the experience of reconciliation, the small group in the church is seen as a primary means of communicating this promise and gift of the gospel, both through words of reconciliation and through reconciling relationships. Nothing that can be done by verbal symbols of theology alone to assure man in his anxiety of God's redemptive acceptance of him is sufficient. Verbal theological assurance alone, whether through preaching, counseling, or formal teaching, does not get at the root of man's need. The layman needs actual emotional acceptance by a concerned group of fellow Christians if the verbal assurances of forgiveness are to have a clear personal meaning for him. Such acceptance on the human side by members of the body of Christ matches what is meant on the divine side by God's justification by grace, and adds a fuller dimension to its meaning.

The ministry of reconciliation, which is the task entrusted both to the minister and to the church as a whole, consists in large measure in the establishment of relationships of mutual acceptance such as are especially possible within the life of small groups. If church members are to be more profoundly and intimately united in fellowship with one another and with Christ, the church will need to provide more face-to-face relationships for its members, where they can associate in small meaningful groups in which Christian truth and Christian experience go hand in hand. Revelation, by its very nature, is personally appropriated, if it is appropriated at all. The adult Christian education program, as an agent for the re-enactment of revelation, must therefore emphasize the personal dimension. It must utilize techniques that foster personal encounter with other individuals as well as with the subject matter of the Christian tradition.

The small study group, as a fellowship of reconciliation, can provide the kinds of personal relationships that are needed to undergird the communication of the Christian message of God's forgiving and reconciling activity. Harold R. Fray, Jr., gives us an example from his own church of how such groups can give reality to this divine message through the unspoken language of relationships:

> There was no question that some members began to see the Christian faith in a new light, and real changes began to take place in their lives. Perhaps the best explanation is that what had been words about the Christian faith was translated by the group into concrete reality. Love, acceptance, forgivenesss, were no longer " halo words," but living experiences in the relationships of the members of the groups. The words literally became incarnate. People felt that they could be themselves without jeopardy. They could witness to their faith or express their doubts without fear.[76]

Nor is the therapeutic potentiality of small groups limited only to creative relationships with other persons; it also includes a creative relationship to one's self. In the very process of fostering the encounter between God and man, small groups are well suited for the revelatory and therapeutic task of increasing self-confrontation and self-understanding. Self-confrontation is an important element in any psychotherapeutic process; and it is also an essential aspect of any Christian experience of revelation, since revelation involves not only an encounter with God within the context of the Christian community, but also encounter with oneself. It is often through group experiences that an individual becomes most fully aware of his deeper needs and of his characteristic ways of meeting them. The creation of the right kind of group atmosphere can result in a beneficial development of one's ability to perceive himself as he is. In the personal interaction of democratic discussion, persons are likely to become aware of the discrepancy between what they fancy their relations with others to be, and what they actually do to other people and what others do to them. Such experiences are important for growth in self-understanding, self-criticism, and self-acceptance, and are therefore of vital significance in attaining one of the chief goals of Christian education. As Lewis J. Sherrill has said, Christian education at its best leads not simply to gnosis, that is, to knowledge *about* God and oneself. It leads also to epignosis, *thorough* knowledge of God and oneself and others as *persons in relationship.*[77]

THERAPEUTIC USE OF THE BIBLE IN SMALL GROUPS

In *The Gift of Power*, Dr. Sherrill provides us with an excellent conceptualization of the relationship between divine revelation and human need. He conceives of the relationship as consisting in man's " call " — his searching and question-raising — and God's " answer." He directly applies this dialogue between divine revelation and human

need, which he finds running through the Bible, to the contemporary relation between the Bible and the layman. Thus
he sees the problem of relevance in Christian education as
a problem of properly correlating divine answers with human questions, Biblical themes with man's basic predicaments, something after the manner of Tillich's " principle
of correlation." For example, he relates the Biblical theme
of divine providence to man's predicament of undiscerned
meaning, i.e., his inability to find a meaningful pattern or
purpose within his life experiences. Similarly, he relates the
Biblical themes of judgment and redemption to man's
estrangement from God, and the theme of God's continual
re-creation to man's estrangement from himself, etc., with
several other major themes.

This conceptual scheme advanced by Sherrill possesses
great merit; for surely our central purpose in using the Bible
in Christian education is to prepare the way for men and
women to perceive and respond to God in the present. The
proper aim of Bible study is to make the divine-human
encounters recorded there both contemporaneous and personal, to bring man's need and God's action together in a
creative, redemptive, and therefore therapeutic dialogue.
Since the major Biblical themes and the predicaments of
man are in correspondence, the materials drawn from the
Bible for use in study groups should be chosen with the
anxieties and other problems of the people of our own time
and place in mind. Such selection, especially when the
group members themselves have a part in it, helps guarantee
the relevance of revelation.

This line of thinking is very different from that so often
voiced by many laymen who want to " learn more about
the Bible " because they virtually equate increasing their
Biblical knowledge with " being a better Christian." Such
a view resembles the Gnostic heresy, so rampant in the first

centuries of the church's life, in its equation of salvation with special religious knowledge. The Bible's own injunctions against every form of idolatry are contradicted by a widespread tendency among our laymen to regard the Bible as a sacred book to be worshiped and studied as an end in itself. It is safe to say that thinking such as this often lies behind the expressed desire to study a particular book in the Bible. Of course, better acquaintance with the content of various books in the Bible is in many ways a very commendable goal. But from the standpoint of achieving greater relevance, an approach to Bible study that seeks to relate particular Biblical themes to particular human predicaments seems more profitable. Most books of the Bible are of limited usefulness in this regard because they contain a rather confusing multiplicity of themes, many of which may be quite irrelevant to the present needs of the group members. The great Biblical themes transcend the contents of any one book of the Bible. Perhaps it is best to begin with the study of a particular book, if that is the consensus of the group. Then the encounter there with fragments of themes which " speak to their condition " may lead them afield into a wider and more systematic exploration of other books of the Bible. This thematic approach to Bible study, relating divine theme to human predicament, is essentially the study of Biblical theology; and it is tremendously rewarding in terms of relevance.

An approach to the Bible that starts from the definition and analysis of human need, from problems identified by the members of a study group, gives a sense of immediacy to the study of the Bible. However, there are dangers in an unduly one-sided approach from the standpoint of needs and problems of which the layman happens to be conscious. It may tend toward a practicalism in the use of the Bible, which would keep the sense of need at a shallow level and obscure a realization of the more profound relevance of the Bible. Laymen may then come to regard the Bible as a sort of handbook or source book, or even as a religious encyclopedia or almanac to be consulted in moments of uncertainty.

The quest for relevance is, of course, commendable; but it may lead to a preoccupation with lesser, tangential needs and problems that misses contact with man's *predicaments*, those *persisting* and often subconscious concerns arising from anxieties over an existence in which every security is threatened sooner or later. To deal with the more easily verbalized and more specific problems and needs of people without recognizing their deeper rootage in the more basic human predicaments is to run the risk of dealing with symptoms while ignoring the more profound anxiety. When this occurs, the revelatory and therapeutic functions of the study group are only superficially fulfilled. The encounter between the layman and the Bible then will not touch the deepest roots of human selfhood or the profoundest aspects of the Biblical message.

Thus an exclusive use of the " problem-centered approach " to Bible study is insufficient. That is why the adult leader must often be one step ahead of the group, introducing Biblical material that may not be relevant to the expressed needs and interests of the group, but that serves instead to bring the group to an awareness of need at a deeper level. When the layman is confronted by the living Word of God, that is, when we bring a Biblical theme to the attention of our laymen instead of relying *exclusively* on the technique of bringing their needs and problems to the Biblical text, often something will be said to them that will have nothing to do with the conscious questions they may be asking. It may be a startlingly profound question that the laymen must now answer. They often discover that instead of searching the Scriptures, the Scriptures are searching them. In the divine-human dialogue of Bible study, they often find that the roles are interchanged; instead of questioning, they are being questioned. In the dialogue between man and God's Word, man not only receives answers to his immediate questions; he also discovers searching divine questions that are directed to the very core of his being, uncovering aspects of his predicament as man that he was not previously aware existed, and driving him to search within the Word and within his own experiences for the corresponding divine answers.

Revelation, as William Temple has aptly defined it, is the result of historical event plus divinely inspired interpretation of the event. Thus, revelation has both a subjective and an objective focus. The use of the Bible as a means of contemporary revelation to our laymen therefore requires of us a dual attention both to the objective Biblical themes and also to subjective human problems and predicaments. We must keep both the objective divine " Thou " and the subjective human " I " in perspective. When either focus of attention is ignored, there is no genuine revelation, even though we may call our activity " Bible study."

Starting Where the Layman Is

In his work with people the minister is always in danger of being irrelevant, of answering questions no one is asking. To avoid this danger, the minister as adult educator must be sensitive to the " cues " contained in the remarks of his laymen, as well as to other guides that reveal their questions and problems. Realistic programs of adult work in the local church cannot be developed without intimate knowledge of the particular situation in which they are to be employed, especially in regard to the particular needs of the laymen. In their life situation, our laymen live in the particular. They can always turn to an interest in the universal when they are trying to find meaning for their lives in a world where they continually discover the immediate and the particular to be disappointing and frustrating. The danger of this interest in the universal, this inclination to broad generalizations, is that it may be a means of escape from the vexing particularities of the problems of home, office, and community. When discussion in a study group is confined to pious generalizations, it lacks the specificity that is necessary for relevance. The adult educator must hold in focus the particularity of his laymen's needs.

This is essential, since effective learning must begin with needs that the learners *recognize* as needs. Of course, in any vital group these recognized needs are never static. The leader must be ready for curriculum change as the members develop a more thorough appraisal of their needs. Groups have begun with the discussion of some Christian doctrine or, as in the case of one men's group, with such a generalized topic as " What Is Life's Meaning? " and have found themselves driven to Bible study. Others have begun with the study of a particular book of the Bible and through this they have discovered a need for more background in Biblical theology. Not only must the leader " start where the layman is," he must be sensitive to subsequent developments in group maturity and interest.

An important corollary of this emphasis on the importance of beginning with conscious needs and interests is that denominational adult curriculum materials can rarely be followed with any exactitude. A completely planned curriculum is an impossibility if the small study group is actually a place of dynamic personal interaction and true two-way communication. The exact direction and rate of progress of such vital groups simply cannot be plotted out by the curriculum writers. The fact that thousands of adult classes across the country are studying the same lesson in their denominational materials is indeed impressive; but the materials may or may not be relevant to the stage of religious development and concern that a particular group has reached. Seldom would there be many groups at identically the same point in their needs. Of course, curriculum units that follow a logical pattern of development over a period of months or years may be of great value as a resource for future reference by study groups in the church. If such material is of high quality, it is always well to order a quantity of it for either present or future use. But the relationship between the present needs of the group and the theme of a current curriculum unit will usually be one of accord only by coincidence, since there is no way to tell except by gross generalizations what the adults of a large group of churches might need as their study materials for a particular series of meetings. Writes Dr. J. Gordon Chamberlain, minister of Christian education in New York's Riverside Church:

> The educator in the church may sympathize with those held responsible by their denominational agencies for producing adult curriculum materials, but his insight and evaluation of " where man is " determines where he will begin and what will be included in the program of education.[78]

The adult educator in the local church is naturally tempted to leave all his curriculum planning up to the curriculum editors, the " wise men in the East," because the material is all prepared for him together with teaching aids of various kinds. The accompanying discussion guides are nearly always useful to some extent; but they can easily become a crutch, or even a means of stifling the natural course of discussion. No discussion guide can ever provide for the almost infinite possibilities of discussion development inherent in a lively group. Many adult groups are needlessly confined to denominational church school curriculum materials because their leaders are afraid to tackle any book or pamphlet that does not provide a neatly packaged discussion guide. Even when these curriculum materials are used, slavish adherence to their procedural outlines is to be avoided. With a little more trust in the power of the Holy Spirit to lead groups of Christians into new truth, these cautious leaders could follow more flexibly the emergent concerns of their groups.

THE IMPORTANCE OF LAY INITIATIVE

Just as it is important to start with the conscious needs and interests of our laymen, so also it is best to have the original impetus for starting study groups come from a layman or group of laymen. Such " spontaneous combustion " has often set many on fire with the idea of adult study more effectively than if the minister had initiated it. In many ways, these other-directed adults of ours respond more readily to suggestions and invitations coming from other laymen.

Ministers may shake their heads in wonder when they hear of the spontaneous origination of study groups in other churches, saying, " I wish that could happen in my church! " Yet more often than not in these churches, laymen have first casually suggested the idea, and the minister has then seized upon this opportunity and encouraged them to gather some of their friends together for an initial group. I have never heard of a church where the origin of such groups could be said to have been *purely* spontaneous. I know of one church that has a set policy that no new group can come into being until the members request this of the minister; but the lay initiative that started the first groups in this church was stimulated by the minister's frequent reference in sermons and personal conversations to the unique spiritual opportunities available in small groups.

The experience of the Montview Boulevard Presbyterian Church in Denver is particularly instructive as an illustration of how lay initiative and pastoral direction may be fruitfully combined. The original group was an outgrowth of a building committee, consisting of the senior minister and several laymen, who had been working together closely for a year. When their formal work was finished, they decided to continue to meet for discussion and study. After a time, the ministers invited any member of the congregation to gather a study group on any topic of interest. Still another method they employed was to approach two or three persons directly and personally with this suggestion. By 1954 there were about thirty adult study groups in the church that had originated largely, but never wholly, on the basis of lay initiative. The minister who is himself convinced of the value of adult study groups will find many ways to communicate his enthusiasm, and he will be quick to encourage every expression of interest that comes from his people. Whenever lay initiative plays a part in the origination of adult study groups, the topic for study is more likely to be something in which the laymen are vitally interested.

GOING BEYOND CONSCIOUS NEEDS AND INTERESTS

When we begin with conscious needs and interests, the autonomous motivation of our laymen is naturally enlisted in the educational enterprise. This provides an immediate focus for study and attention. Herein lies the value of the " interest finder " or the " fad principle," whereby the fad of the moment determines the direction of study and discussion.

However, there are definite drawbacks to the exclusive use of interest finders and other techniques of a similar nature for determining the content of adult Christian education. People check an interest finder on the basis of ephemeral interests in the particular items listed before them, and in terms of the conscious motivations of the moment. It is quite likely that such techniques will not bring to light the deeper and often unconscious needs of adults, such as their need for security and acceptance and a more profound understanding of life's meaning. Revelation consists, as we have seen, in God's confrontation of man and man's response to the encounter. Consequently, a philosophy of adult Christian education that gives a central place to revelation will emphasize the confrontation of adults by that which will draw forth the deeper questions they may not now be asking.

From this point of view it is easy to see how completely unsatisfactory it is simply to catalogue the topics people say they want to explore, and then to determine the direction of study solely with this as a guide. The minister as adult educator cannot assume that what his laymen are " interested " in is all they need to study. Adults do not fully know what they want to learn until they have begun to encounter subject matter that transcends their immediate, conscious interests and that, also, is related to their deepest needs. If the material with which the adult educator confronts the layman is truly relevant to his needs, it will establish its own point of contact with him. The very " givenness " of the Christian message confronts the educator, and he in turn is responsible for confronting the learner with it.

In these days when the term " content-centered " has become almost a derisive epithet in many educational circles, it is well for the Christian educator to remind himself that he is responsible for the continued recital of God's saving acts and the transmission of the subject matter of the historical faith and life of the Christian church. The continuing encounter, through which revelation is personally appropriated, is partially dependent upon the teaching method of challenge and confrontation with material not directly suggested by the layman. Confrontation as an educational method means the intentional confronting of individuals with facts or experiences that challenge them, bringing them to more significant levels of encounter with the subject matter of the Christian faith.

This is far more than simply a matter of confronting learners with questions intended to elicit merely factual answers. It is somewhat akin to " reality-testing " in psychotherapy in that it challenges the members of the group not to apply pious generalizations to specific cases and situations in which they are personally involved. It is a matter of leading the group from " peripheral responses " to " depth responses." As the group perceives new truths and insights of a general nature, the leader summarizes or restates them, and proposes leading questions that challenge and stimulate the group to see the deeper and more personal implications of these discoveries for their lives. Mountain-top experiences of spiritual insight often occur in the lives of groups; but they can easily become plateaus of premature satisfaction. The teaching method of challenge and confrontation is a way of shaking a group out of its complacency, stirring its members to dissatisfaction with the point of development they have reached as individuals and as a group. An example of the way in which groups can get sidetracked into fairly superficial discussions may be seen in the great interest they often show in the beliefs and practices of other denominations, and particularly of the sects. Often discussion along these lines will serve no other purpose than to satisfy their curiosity. If the members of the group do not suggest it themselves, the leader should challenge the group to perceive spiritual strengths in the witness of the sects and of other denominations that are a judgment upon their own discipleship.

The minister as adult leader has a greater function to perform than simply that of helping a group to define its problems and areas of concern as the members see them, and helping them select and clarify their group goals strictly in accordance with their conscious needs and interests. As a theologian, he has a doctrine of man and of man's ultimate predicaments and needs that usually transcends the group's appraisals. If he takes his theology seriously, he cannot in good conscience adopt a laissez-faire attitude toward the dynamic process whereby needs and interests are formulated by the group. He will use every possible resource, from the Bible to contemporary literature and social issues, to challenge the group toward an awareness of the profounder theological dimensions of their needs. They must be led to participate in a theological diagnosis of their common plight as men and women afflicted with estrangement and the anxiety of meaninglessness and other haunting concerns before they will earnestly seek any remedy for their soul-sickness in the Christian gospel.

AUTHORITARIANISM IN THE STUDY GROUP

A realistic philosophy of adult Christian education must come to grips with the problem of authoritarianism in the role expectations of both the laymen and the minister. We must remember that the learning patterns of the adult — the ways in which he knows *how* to learn — reflect in large measure the ways in which he learned as a child. As Charles K. Ferguson points out in an article in *Adult Leadership*, the average adult tends to expect his adult class to resemble the usually authoritarian class atmosphere he has known in grade school, high school, or college.[79] He expects to be told, and regards himself as essentially a passive listener. This is especially true in the church. The people look to the minister as the authority figure who is to " tell " them. From their point of view, the minister's authority consists primarily in his greater religious knowledge. He is the " religious expert " who is to preach to them, to lecture to them, and they are to remain passive and silent.

We can expect this " clamming up " to be especially obvious in the first few meetings of an adult group. And the adults will continue to remain passive unless or until the minister as adult leader takes steps to redefine his role in the group so as to alter the authoritarian role expectations that his people hold in regard to his function. Unless this is done, the voluntary adult study group in the church will be " voluntary " only in the sense that people come to it of their own volition; there is nothing " voluntary " about an authoritarian group atmosphere except the amazing willingness of adults to submit to it!

Adorno, the social psychologist, has shown through extensive experimentation that we can expect an authoritarian environment to produce either submissive or dominating behavior. Indeed, both of these behavioral extremes are common in many groups. The submissive adult will be afraid of discovering and expressing his genuine convictions. He will remain silent concerning differences of opinion or questions he may have for fear of appearing ignorant. The dominating adult, on the other hand, will aggressively seek to impose his opinions on others. In either case, creative interaction cannot take place. Submissive and dominating behavior among the group members can be expected to develop in direct proportion to the degree of authoritarianism in the leader's approach.

The layman quite naturally projects the role of religious

expert on the minister, and this in turn is often reinforced by the minister's own image of himself and of his function in the group. A factor making it very hard for the expert *as such* to be democratic and to switch from the role of formal instructor to the role of discussion leader, is his admittedly greater knowledge and the fact that he so often conceives of his essential function as that of enlightening the group by "telling" them. On the basis of their personal observations in discussion leadership classes they have conducted across the country, Harry A. and Bonaro W. Overstreet state that those who have the hardest time learning to be good discussion leaders are teachers and ministers. Their previous training and experience, the Overstreets declare, condition them to do nearly all the talking.[80] The minister's special knowledge is in a sense a serious handicap. It is hard for him when leading a discussion group to restrain himself when he "knows the answer."

Even when he is able to restrain himself from giving the answer that comes so easily to him because of his theological training, he is often tempted to turn a group discussion into a guessing game. He strives to guide the group to the "right answer" by fishing for the ideas and even the specific words he wants to hear, rapidly asking questions that are likely to be answerable only by a yes or a no. He may be so intent on eliciting the exact response he wants that he cuts short or overlooks contributions that reflect important doubts or insights. Often he will consider this process to be a democratic group discussion, when actually it is little more than a catechetical exercise or examination. This is a way of using group discussion as a "developmental teaching method" all right; that is, it allows people to develop the point the leader wishes to get across by manipulating their responses so as to arrive at a rigidly preconceived result.

When the minister functions as a resource person in a group, whether in addition to or in distinction from the role of discussion leader, his special knowledge poses another barrier to democratic participation. Usually his factual religious *knowledge* and his personal theological *interpretation* of these facts are so closely and automatically related in his thinking that it is difficult for him not to give *both* fact *and* interpretation of the fact when he acts as a resource person. But when he gives his theological interpretations immediately along with the facts the group needs, he deprives the group of the opportunity of discovering the personal significance of the factual material by working out an interpretation themselves. If revelation truly consists in the interplay between experiential or historical fact and Spirit-inspired interpretation, it can only occur in the group if the leader allows and encourages the group to work out its own interpretation of the facts he supplies. Revelation becomes a reality for the learners only when such processes of personal interpretation are part of their response.

The wealth of knowledge that the minister possesses also tempts him to present everything he knows that pertains to a question the group may direct at him. He must discipline himself to select and present only those items of information which the group needs at a given time, and to give such information as concisely as possible. It is admittedly difficult for a leader who does have special knowledge to avoid becoming the group's only resource person. Most groups are quite willing to put their minister in this role, neglecting the resources possessed by the group members. The minister must not allow himself to be forced into the role of speechmaker, the one who answers every question that arises. If he does, he may find himself doing the whole job, to the detriment of the development of group responsibility and mature independence.

One of the chief problems the minister faces as an adult educator is the problem of finding the means of reducing the prestige differential between himself and his laymen so that he can assume a less authoritarian role in the group. But he must first reduce it in his *own* mind before he can reduce it in the minds of his laymen; and this is often very hard to do. Few of us are willing to admit or are capable of perceiving the degree to which we seek to dominate others. To be an authority, dispensing crumbs of religious knowledge to the multitudes, is a very ego-satisfying role. Our position is a cherished reward for years of study. Modifying our teaching methods toward the encouragement of more group participation involves some degree of threat to our status. Our laymen may then no longer regard us as omniscient. Encouraging more group participation will mean that more embarrassing questions are likely to be raised, less emphasis will be placed on learning directly from us, and our leadership may be challenged by aggressive, intelligent laymen. Thus our knowledge of the techniques of group dynamics theory will not alone suffice in reducing our prestige differential; for we shall not earnestly and wholeheartedly employ such techniques for altering our laymen's authoritarian role expectations or for combating our temptations to authoritarianism unless we have convinced ourselves on theological grounds of the importance of doing this.

The minister as " religious expert " needs to remind himself of the theological fact that just as he confronts his learners with the facts of revelation, so he himself is confronted by them. In this sense, the leader and the learner stand side by side in the group as they are confronted together by God's Word. And there is another theological point we should keep in mind. H. Richard Niebuhr reminds us that:

> The infinitely active and inexhaustible nature of the subjects of theology reduces to relatively small significance the distance between the more and less mature members of the community of inquiry. Teachers and students form one group before their common objects, which are, indeed, subjects actively making their presence felt in the community.[81]

Niebuhr is speaking here of the relationship between seminary professors and students; but what he says is equally true of the relationship between the minister and his laymen. The theological recognition of our involvement with our laymen as objects of God's revealing activity, together with a realization of our relative equality in ignorance before the divine mysteries, will do much to dispel the notions of " expertness " that lead to authoritarianism.

If we conceive our primary purpose as adult educators to be that of making up for deficiencies in the religious knowledge our laymen possess, then naturally we will feel our anxiety heightened when persons ask us questions we cannot answer at the moment for lack of information. We will tend to restrict the functioning of the group in order to avoid this kind of situation. But if we continually remind ourselves of the inexhaustible depth and complexity of Christian truth and keep in mind the fact that our primary function is not to be " answer men " but guides through areas that only the mind of God can fully comprehend, we shall then have both the wisdom and the humility to say on occasion, " I don't know," or " There is no single absolute answer to that question." We will not be embarrassed by questions we cannot answer immediately or simply, since we will be able freely to admit our fallibility and finitude without worrying about a loss of status.

CHAPTER SEVEN:

A Second Look at Group Dynamics Theory

GROUP DYNAMICS THEORY AND CHRISTIAN KOINŌNIA

THERE is no question but that at many points group dynamics theory may be utilized to further the kind of group life that should exist in the church. In many ways, its compatibility with the Christian concept of *koinōnia* is evident. J. Robert Nelson writes in his highly significant book on the nature of the church, *The Realm of Redemption*, "Most scholars are agreed that the fundamental idea which *koinōnia* conveys is that of 'participation in something in which others also participate.'" [82] *Koinōnia*, as it is used in the New Testament, does not mean simply "fellowship" in the limited sense of mere association with others. Its meaning, according to Nelson, is better signified by such words as "a sharing," "a joint possession," "a participation," "a holding in common." [83] Such qualities of interaction as these are among the central objectives of group dynamics theory.

Those who are anxious to "get on with the subject" to which a group has committed itself often feel that group dynamics theory is too permissive concerning the verbal content of the interaction. But at least in the initial development of a new learning group some apparently purposeless and superficial conversation is often helpful in developing freedom of expression — an important consideration in view of the authoritarian expectations our adults have been conditioned to bring along with them. Group participants often need to feel free to talk in impersonal terms or to trade platitudes for a few meetings before they can feel free to trust one another with their more personal opinions, insights, doubts, and misunderstandings. Until there is mutual trust, there can be no significant mutual sharing; and without such sharing, there can be little embodiment in the group of what the New Testament means by *koinōnia*.

Any technique that enhances participation in group discussion helps provide laymen with various necessary Christian disciplines, such as subjecting one's opinions to the corrective judgment of others, identifying oneself with the lives and problems of others, speaking with candor and integrity, and working co-operatively with others for a common goal. Group dynamics theory places much emphasis upon various techniques that encourage full group participation. On the basis of what was said earlier concerning the nature of revelation as a phenomenon requiring the participation and interaction of a community of persons, an important test of any method is whether or not it facilitates two-way communication. In this regard, the relevance of group dynamics theory to the process of revelation through small groups is quite clear.

Group dynamics theory also places great emphasis on formal group disciplines. It is opposed to any authoritarian attempt by a leader to impose such disciplines and requirements, or to suggest or encourage participants to adopt them before they are ready. Group disciplines should always be a matter of group consensus, and as a group matures it may adopt new ones. However, group dynamics theorists maintain there are certain disciplines that the group must accept from the very start if it is to be truly a group and not merely an aggregation of people. Certain disciplines are essential to group cohesiveness. The group members must agree to attend faithfully for a stated number of sessions and to assume personal responsibility for whatever outside reading or other preparation is decided upon by the group. Regular attendance and responsible preparation are basic disciplines without which the group members cannot hope to grow steadily and consistently in the quantity and quality of their participation. The church, too, has always maintained that various self-imposed disciplines are essential for spiritual growth.

It is difficult to imagine how a study group in the church could function as a vital influence upon its members without these minimal disciplines of regular attendance and outside preparation. And as the cohesiveness of a group develops, the members may decide to give this cohesiveness fuller expression through additional disciplines such as periods of silence and daily prayer. Group disciplines can be a means of both expressing and furthering group solidarity, even when they are observed privately outside the actual group situation. Self-imposed disciplines have always played a part in the life of creative groups in the church. There is an important sense in which " law " must precede " gospel " in the history of a group even as it did in Biblical history; there must be commitment to basic group disciplines before life in the group can lead to increased commitment to Christ. However, group dynamics theory is correct in insisting that such disciplines be self-imposed. One of the first signs of decay in the vitality of any group is to be seen when group disciplines cease to be based on group consensus. That is what happened, for example, to what had originally been the almost spontaneous disciplines of the old Methodist class meetings. The proper application of group dynamics theory is an important safeguard against any external legalism in the matter of group disciplines.

Group dynamics theory is also consistent with the Protestant principle of the priesthood of all believers, or, to use
a more current expression, the "ministry of the laity."
Luther's idea of the Christian layman being ideally a
"Christ to his neighbor," or "putting on the neighbor,"
certainly implies the principle that the layman is to be an
agent of revelation, a minister of reconciliation, to his
brother in Christ. This principle is served by the emphasis
in group dynamics theory upon rotating, reciprocal, and
emergent leadership in the group. This stress on group responsibility, through emergent lay leadership and through
participation based on responsible preparation, approaches
in group life something of what is meant by the idea of the
ministry of the laity.

A corollary of these concepts of the ministry of the laity
and emergent group leadership is that the minister will seek
to work himself out of the role of leader and into the role
of member and occasional resource person as rapidly as the
emotional and intellectual maturity of the group will allow.
This principle of complete involvement with the group on
the part of the minister is in accord with the idea that the
minister not only confronts his people with the Word, but
also is himself confronted by it. As Daniel Jenkins declares
in *The Gift of Ministry:*

> Surely it is of the essence of the priestly function of the
> ministry that . . . the minister is, as their representative,
> one of the people, identified with them in the closest pos-
> sible way. To deny that, or to minimize it is, apart from
> any other considerations, to deny all that is involved in
> our Lord's real identification with our common man-
> hood.[84]

The minister, who is himself being confronted by the
Word, does not become one who does something to other

people, or one who tries to make something happen to them, while he himself remains untouched. Rather, he continues to learn, along with his laymen, and to open himself to the healing, transforming power of the fellowship of which he is a part.

Group dynamics theory can become a spiritual instrument by fostering the total involvement of the minister within the dynamics of group interaction. The demonic element appears when the minister as leader is not himself involved in the group process, for then he is tempted to use the techniques of group dynamics theory as a means of manipulating others. When the minister, so to speak, " stands outside " the group process, he may be totally unaware of the fact that he is manipulating the responses of his laymen. In this way, an apparently democratic group atmosphere may become a demonic disguise under cover of which the minister unwittingly succumbs to the temptations of authoritarianism.

One of the best ways for the minister to avoid the temptation to misuse group dynamics theory is for him to have a previous experience of involvement in a small Christian fellowship group. How can he hope to guide others into something he has not himself experienced? It is very difficult for him to have an experience of total involvement in a group composed of laymen. He can never break loose completely from the role of religious *leader*, which he is so accustomed to assume around laymen and which the laymen in turn always will expect him to assume to some degree. He cannot have in such a group the experience of being a *member* on a completely equal plane with other members. Only in a fellowship group with other ministers, where the distinction between clergyman and laymen can be avoided, can he fully participate in the sort of experience toward which he would lead his laymen. Herein lies the wisdom of the Church Officer Training Program of The United Presbyterian Church U.S.A. Ministers are discouraged from using the officer training materials until they have first attended regional preparatory conferences. At these conferences, they are assigned to small discussion groups under the leadership of men who have received special training in group dynamics theory as well as in the content of the material. In these groups, the ministers have some foretaste of what they can lead their laymen to experience. Similarly, Paul Bergevin and John McKinley, the developers of the Indiana Plan for Adult Religious Education which is being used in many Episcopal churches, stress the importance of having the ministers of churches considering using the plan attend a district training institute where the plan is not only explained but experienced in training sessions in group dynamics theory.

The minister who has participated in a small fellowship of other ministers where group dynamics techniques are applied will be able to employ them much more fruitfully than if he has only done some reading in the field of group dynamics theory. Without this experience, or something similar to it, it is all too easy for the minister to slip into old authoritarian modes of leadership even though intellectually he may know better. Like Paul, he may find that he " can will what is right," but that he " cannot do it " (Rom. 7:18, RSV). Previous group experience of the right kind can help him do what he knows is right in group leadership.

In group dynamics theory, " feedback " is a term used to denote any method by which the quantity and quality of group interaction is observed and later " fed back " to the group for careful consideration. Often this is accomplished by assigning one person to be a group observer, to take notes on what was said and who said it, and then to present an evaluative summary and report on group participation near the end of the meeting. This emphasis on critical evaluation and " feedback " in group dynamics theory is harmonious with the idea of Christian *koinōnia* as a fellowship that provides for judgment and forgiveness, criticism and acceptance. Evaluation involves humility and self-criticism on the part of the group members as well as the leader. It accords well with the theological conviction that all persons stand under God's judgment, and that God often speaks his word of judgment through human words of criticism.

" Feedback " may serve effectively as a vehicle of judgment upon the whole group, particularly on the quality of personal interaction within it. That is why the idea of having a group observer is not just another gimmick, even though in many groups it would not be essential or even desirable to have one. This method of " feedback " may be an unnecessarily mechanical way to evaluate the quality of group interaction; but such evaluation, whether it comes through an observer or more informally through the comments of the members, solicited and encouraged by the leader, can play a vital role in the development of better relationships within the group.

Finally, we must recognize that group dynamics theory is useful in helping the layman to overcome some of the major problems he faces in modern social life, as these were outlined in an earlier chapter. It serves to counteract some of the destructive effects of depersonalization in the layman's work and social relations, and the decline of meaningful and intimate voluntary associations in our society. It also combats the twofold authoritarian tendencies of both needing to dominate others and needing to lose one's self and one's control to a power that carries one along.

Both tendencies are destructive of human selfhood, and any techniques that counteract them may be said to serve the purposes of the gospel of redemption.

THE LIMITATIONS OF GROUP DYNAMICS THEORY

Years ago, when audio-visual materials were first coming into widespread use in the churches, many people hailed them as the coming of the kingdom for Christian education. It took years of actual experience to tone down the general enthusiasm for audio-visual methods to more realistic proportions. Today, there seems to be a similar tendency to regard group dynamics theory as the perfect panacea for the problems of Christian education, and of adult education in particular. We must remind ourselves that group dynamics techniques, like audio-visual materials, are only another set of tools for Christian education. Like all tools, these techniques have their limitations.

No educational method is sacrosanct. For the Christian educator, it is only the *content* which he would communicate and not the *methods* he uses which possesses this ultimacy. Experience has shown that no one teaching method is always and invariably superior to all others. Tests have shown that learning is as much related to the particular personality structure of the learner as it is to methods of teaching. Some people learn better under one method, others learn better under another. The adult educator must be ready to use a variety of methods even in small groups, which are admittedly best suited for the method of group discussion. Occasions will arise in such groups when the best method may be the introduction of new factual material or the clarification of a point by means of audio-visuals, oral reading from some authoritative source, or a talk by a well-informed outside speaker. Only the employment of a variety of methods can prevent a group from falling into a rigid pattern such as spelled the demise of the Methodist class meetings, or such as so often stultifies the traditional adult church school class.

Educational work with adults in small groups simply cannot be confined to group discussion, even though we fully acknowledge its great value as an educational method and its accordance with the principle of *koinōnia*. Both leader and learner are confronted with the " givenness " of revelation in the content of the Bible and of Christian history, doctrine, and tradition. This givenness implies that the leader as resource person must supplement group discussion with the presentation of factual " stimulus material," which for one reason or another is not readily available to the great majority of the people in the group, if the discussion is to be more than a pooling of ignorance on many points.

A good example of a situation that should not be controlled entirely by the dynamics of group discussion is the communicants class. The minister has only a limited number of meetings in which he has the responsibility of seeing to it that the group covers certain salient aspects of Christian doctrine and of the practices and traditions of the church. Unless he controls the course of the discussion, these people may not be adequately prepared for church membership. Here is an instance where it is best to fit the individual to the curriculum, instead of fitting the curriculum to the individual in accordance with group dynamics theory; for a certain minimal body of religious knowledge is essential for intelligent churchmanship.

In every study group situation, the minister as leader and as servant of the Word is responsible for its kerygmatic declaration if there is to be genuine encounter between the Word and man. But confrontation with the Word is often an unsettling experience, because it constantly throws our present way of thinking and living into question. The natural course of group discussion will often tend away from the content of the Christian message, toward a " safer " discussion of personal experiences and observations quite unrelated to it. It is the responsibility of the discussion leader, because of his ultimate concern for the communication of the content of the Christian message, to maintain some control over these digressions. If the opinions and feelings and experiences expressed by the group members are related to the Christian learning goals of the group, the leader should help the group perceive this relationship. Where such digressions are irrelevant, it is incumbent upon the leader to make the participants aware of this irrelevance without needlessly arousing the hostility of any contributor, and to redirect the flow of discussion along more fruitful channels.

It must be recognized that too exclusive an emphasis on the free dynamics of group discussion may lead either to fruitless rambling, or to a preoccupation with procedural and emotional problems to the point where the objective content of the Christian message is neglected and the group members become almost morbid in their introspections and confessions. The " hidden agenda " of thoughts and feelings that our people bring to group meetings is, of course, very important; but it must be supplemented with and guided by the agenda of " God's mighty acts," which meets and answers the needs and questions contained in the " hidden agenda."

As an educational method, group dynamics theory tends to focus attention almost exclusively on the process of verbal interaction between people, often to the detriment of concern for the quality of the ideas being discussed. For example, the Indiana Plan for Adult Religious Education is almost exclusively concerned with participative training of laymen in the practice of group dynamics theory. It virtually ignores the problem of relating participation to content. According to the plan, the first four meetings of the lay training group are devoted to training in group dynamics theory and practice, and content is to be introduced in the next dozen or so meetings primarily to help illustrate the functioning of the group process. Training in techniques of group leadership and group participation comes first. After this, these trainees are to form the nucleus of leaders and participants for a program of adult education in the church, which will *then* give more attention to content.

The philosophy behind this plan seems to be that new attitudes and relationships are to be developed *first*, in virtual abstraction from the content of the Christian faith, and then content will be more easily and fully acquired when people possess these new attitudes and relationships. This is tantamount to saying to the laymen in their alienation and estrangement, " First get reconciled to one another through the utilization of these techniques, and then you may get down to the business of studying the Christian gospel of reconciliation." Actually, the message and the experience of reconciliation and redemption belong together; they cannot be arranged in temporal sequence, least of all in a sequence that places the achievement of reconciliation prior to confrontation with the message of reconciliation. And one wonders whether such groups can ever subsequently break free from all the procedural trivia of blackboards, questionnaires, participation evaluation sheets, and the like for serious study of the content of the Christian faith. The emphasis on group dynamics techniques in the Indiana Plan seems to result in such a preoccupation with subjective reactions to the content that the group will never get around to exploring the content itself.

This is a part of the description of how the training groups are to function according to the Indiana Plan:

> These discussion training groups do not meet to argue or debate doctrines, or to question the beliefs of Christianity. It is not a process of proving the beliefs to be valid or determining what they are. For example, a training group would not set out to discuss " Was Christ Divine? " They might, however, discuss " How Can I Better Understand Christ's Divinity? " and " How Is Christ's Divinity Significant to Me? " It is a process in which people share together in order to enrich the beliefs in their own terms so as to make them more meaningful in everyday living.[85]

But can Christian attitudes and relationships be developed in a vacuum, in isolation from the Christian message, which is their only true source? It is questionable whether a group can discuss intelligently the personal significance of a particular Christian belief until they have first determined the content of that belief.

Group dynamics theory often seems to regard active verbal participation as virtually an end in itself. But mere sociality does not necessarily lead to spiritual growth; rather, it can easily become a substitute for it. Group dynamics theory has effectively demonstrated the barriers to learning that are erected by a *leader's* excessive verbalism; *but it can be justly criticized for encouraging excessive verbalism among the group members themselves.* A person should feel free to remain silent if he so desires without being made to feel that he is " letting the group down." It is one thing to provide a permissive atmosphere in which one can feel free to contribute orally if he so wishes; it is quite another for the leader or other group members to manipulate a response from him. Nor is it essential that all needs and doubts and questions and insights be verbalized in the group. It is often enough if the group process has aided the individual in bringing them to the conscious level where he is *capable* of verbalizing them for himself, and thus can deal with them creatively. Regardless of the atmosphere of trust and acceptance that may exist in a group, there are aspects of one's personal life that should be opened to others, if at all, only with the greatest discretion and reverence. A compulsive emphasis in a group on verbalizing every level of thought and feeling may impel an individual to reveal things he may later regret having revealed.

A study group in the church is not merely an exercise in group therapy, although it certainly is that. But whereas group dynamics theorists tend to confine their vision of the therapeutic potentialities of the group to the process of personal interaction itself, the Christian educator sees therapeutic potentialities also in the interaction between the Christian content of the discussion and the learner, in the confluence of transcendent theme with immanent predicament, objective confrontation with subjective encounter. The Christian educator therefore must recognize not only the therapeutic value but also and especially the *authority* of the content of his curriculum in a way quite different from a secular approach to the authority of any given content. He is not concerned simply with two-way communication between leader and learners in the group situation. Instead of a series of dialogues, he is concerned with a *trialogue* among the leader, the learners, and the authoritative, living Christian content that derives its life and vitality from the Holy Spirit who indwells both it and the members of the group. Genuine therapy of the *soul*, actual *revelation*, occurs within this *trialogue* of leader, learners, and Spirit-infused content.

Although the Christian educator will seek to resist temp-

tations to authoritarianism in group leadership, he differs
from the secular group dynamics theorist in that he cannot
minimize the authority of the Christian content of group
study. He will, of course, utilize group dynamics techniques as a means of transferring authority from the leader
to the learners as far as this is possible. He will also use
these techniques to help create a permissive group environment so that members will feel free to express doubts and
raise questions concerning the content as the group seeks
to enter into creative dialogue with it. Yet he must part
company with secular group dynamics theory in insisting
on the ultimate authority of the content that is the object
of the group's study, and in maintaining that his attribut-
ing ultimacy to the content need not result in an authoritarian climate in the group. The ascription of ultimate authority to the leader in an authoritarian group is, of course,
idolatrous; but it is no less idolatrous to ascribe ultimate
authority to the process of group dynamics or the conclu-
sions reached through it. In the *trialogue* among leader,
learners, and the Christian message, only the latter can be
our final authority, " our ultimate concern," to use Tillich's phrase.

The idea of the group process as a *trialogue* within a
Christian study group points to the distinctive feature of
Christian fellowship that transcends secular group dynamics theory. The latter, as we have seen, is at many points
quite in harmony with the Christian concept of *koinōnia*,
and may be used to help the group fulfill its function as a
Christian fellowship of learning. But the *trialogue* that occurs within true Christian fellowship or *koinōnia* cannot
be included within any purely secular theory of group dynamics, because it is three-dimensional. The idea of *koinōnia* points to a dimension beyond human community, to
a community of divine-human encounter as the locus of

Christian revelation, and, therefore, of Christian education. *Koinōnia*, in the New Testament sense, is a fellowship or participation in the *Holy Spirit*.[86] Therefore, communication in the Christian community is not primarily dependent upon our human ability to communicate, as secular group dynamics theory would assert.

The primary author of the effective transmission of the Christian message is the Holy Spirit, and the minister as leader and communicator must remind himself that the Spirit is his ultimate dependence, and that it should likewise be the ultimate dependence of the entire group. As Hendrik Kraemer has said:

> Communication of the gospel, although it certainly has much in common with the universal phenomenon of communication between men, cannot be regarded as *one* of the many forms of communication. It is a category *sui generis*, at least theologically speaking. It is not simply communication between two partners, but the invisible third partner, the Holy Spirit, is the chief one. The peculiar character and place of communication of the Christian message appears in the fact that its inherent aim is not *persuasion*, however persuasive the act of communication may be, as has to be the case with all communication between men, but *conversion*.[87]

The work of conversion may surely be accomplished within a study group; but it is the work of the Holy Spirit, and not of the group techniques of men, even though the latter may be of use in preparing a suitable environment for the divine-human encounter.

Because secular group dynamics theory does not make room for the Spirit in its scheme of things, it often urges upon the group and its leaders attitudes and behavior that constitute impossible demands without the empowering grace of the Spirit. An example of this is the moralistic admonition that leaders and group members are to be " permissive " and " accepting," as if this were a simple human possibility, a matter of volition alone. Actually, of course, we cannot fully and perfectly accept anyone, even though much of the literature on group dynamics theory implies that acceptance within a group can be achieved simply as a decision of the human will. Underlying this typical thinking of group dynamics theorists is a naïve optimism concerning the nature of man and the power of reason alone to alter human relationships. We must realize that to command or suggest to another the obligation of perfect acceptance is to lay an intolerable legalistic burden upon him.

The real source of the ability to accept others is the personal experience of reconciliation, of justification by faith. Only a sense of personal security born of God's acceptance of us can enable us to help our neighbor, to accept him and his need for acceptance. " Acceptance," " empathy," and " identification " with others, key concepts in group dynamics theory, can only be achieved as our grateful response to the incarnation, God's act of empathy and identification with us. The group can become a permissive fellowship of acceptance and reconciliation only when, through the Holy Spirit, its leaders and members know themselves to be accepted by God. As Reuel Howe has said:

> The Holy Spirit, who brings into *being* the fellowship of love and reconciliation through that same relationship, provides the experience that causes us to *become reconciled* and to *be reconcilers*. . . . Thus, the Spirit gives the relationship in which meaningful communication takes place. The Spirit, therefore, makes our relationship a language, a means of engendering being and communicating meaning. . . . I need grace to be in order to help others to become.[88]

The story of the Tower of Babel is a symbol of the fact that the breakdown of communication is as much a result of the alienation and estrangement caused by *sin* as it is of bad techniques of group dynamics; and the experience of Pentecost is a reminder in symbolic form of the fact that the restoration of communication is at least as dependent upon the reconciling activity of the Holy Spirit as it is upon the employment of effective group techniques. The power of the Holy Spirit can enable us to fulfill in some measure those wise counsels of group dynamics theory which otherwise are mere counsels of perfection, making us the more anxious because we cannot by ourselves fulfill them.

CHAPTER EIGHT:

Some Implications for Local Church Organization

WE HAVE seen that in the traditions of Protestant theology, the central purpose of the church and its ministry is to fulfill the function of teaching, broadly defined, and that this traditional priority of the teaching function is relevant to the needs and problems of both the ministry and the laity today. We have also seen the importance of discharging this function primarily through small groups in the church, although the ministry to the individual and to the entire congregation through other ministerial roles may also be regarded as aspects of the educational role. In everything he does, the minister is to seek to communicate the Word of God to man in his need so that the church may be served by the Word in order that it may become corporately the servant of the Word.

We have seen what this line of thinking implies in ordering and carrying out the various functions of the ministry. We have also examined some of the implications for educational content, method, and program, that follow from an analysis of the needs and problems of our laymen and of the potentialities of small study groups. In this concluding chapter, we shall bring together some of these passing references concerning educational program along with some further implications for parish organization and program that follow from the general philosophy of adult Christian education that has been set forth. These are only stated as generalizations. It is impossible to get very specific without becoming irrelevant, since no two parish situations are identical. That is why a so-called " practical " or how-to-do-it approach that spelled out all the details of a plan for parish organization and program would immediately betray itself as being quite *impractical*. The detailed plans for the organization and expansion of an adult education program must be worked out by each church in terms of its specific situation. Therefore no attempt is made to present a detailed blueprint, but only an architect's sketch as it were, tracing the general outlines of a church that sought to put some of these principles of adult Christian education into practice.

Church Officers

In most Protestant churches, lay officers such as deacons and elders have a right to a seat in nearly all the governing bodies of the denomination, and in the local church they often have an equal voice with the minister, at least in principle, in the administration of all its affairs. This includes questions of doctrine, discipline, legislation, and administration. It is utterly absurd to assume that these men can intelligently participate in these sacred responsibilities without specific preparation for them; and it is hypocritical, to say the least, to ask them to respond affirmatively to questions posed in a service of ordination or dedication or recognition concerning the polity and beliefs of their church when they have never studied them. The trustees of the church likewise need training, not so much in how to conduct their business as in the Christian norms of stewardship and churchmanship, which should govern the conduct of all church business. The United Presbyterian Church

U.S.A. provides an excellent Church Officer Training Program in a three-year cycle, corresponding to the three-year term of office in Presbyterian polity. The yearly themes are " The Nature of the Church," " The Order of the Church," and " The Nurture of the Church." Governing bodies in churches of other denominations will find the materials for the first and third year of the cycle easily adaptable to their own officer training program. Surely, at least the first half hour of each meeting of the official boards of a church could profitably be devoted to a discussion based on these materials, together with other materials related to their specific responsibilities.

The minister is responsible for seeing to it that the teachers in the church school and the lay advisers who assist him with the youth program receive adequate training. Usually there will be people in every parish as well or even better qualified than the minister for conducting training in teaching methods. However, the minister is best qualified for giving his teachers background information that relates to the content of the curriculum. If he conscientiously discharges this function, church school staff meetings, which so often tend to be exclusively concerned with administrative and procedural matters, can become vital study groups in their own right.

Obviously, the minister cannot hope to train church officers and teachers and other leaders in every phase of their work, but he can lead them to appropriate the wealth of printed resources that are available. To this end, he should seek to develop an excellent church library, containing books not only for church officers and teachers but for the entire congregation as well. Richard Baxter's admonition that it is the pastor's responsibility to see that religious books find their way into the home is as relevant a reminder to us today as it was in the seventeenth century. Only if the church has an adequate reference library can the minister delegate to his laymen a steadily increasing amount of responsibility as leaders and resource persons in their study groups and other aspects of the church program. A church library is essential if the teaching ministry of the church is to become in large measure the " ministry of the laity " to one another.

Retreats with the officers of the local church, and with other laymen for that matter, afford worth-while opportunities for worship, fellowship, planning, and study which cannot be equaled in any other way. The churches are just beginning to discover the value of retreats, especially for the adult education program. If the thesis is correct that adult Christian education is best achieved through work with small groups, the prolonged group experience and the shared life of a weekend retreat certainly deserves greater attention. Dr. Gerald Jud, who conducts an extensive program of retreats in his church, has this to say about them:

> Many times retreatants report that their experience in the small discussion group was especially helpful; some even say that it is the high point of the retreat for them. . . . One of the most significant by-products of these discussion groups is that once a person gets a taste of the joy of creative group discussion in the realm of his faith, it is very easy to lead that person into one of the established study groups in the church.[89]

The minister who never makes a retreat to a secluded spot with some of his laymen except for the annual Sunday school picnic is missing a great opportunity for intensive adult Christian education.

Earlier we noted that all too often the voluntary adult organizations of the church are quite unrelated to one another, and that the secular nature of the programs of many of these organizations is often attributable to the failure of the minister to see his teaching function as including service to these organizations as a resource person in program-planning. There is a definite need for an adult education council under the church's committee on Christian education, including in its membership the program chairmen of these organizations. Within this council the minister can help adults achieve greater co-ordination between their organizational programs and at the same time a closer correlation between these programs and the central purposes of the church, as he leads them into deeper insights concerning this. These program planners must have an adequate doctrine of the church before they can adequately evaluate their own programs and make wise selections. We all realize the extent to which our churches already tend to be overorganized. We should first work to transform the program content of existing adult organizations in the church, adding new groups only where necessary to meet our people's deepest needs.

Communicants Classes

It would be difficult to overemphasize the importance of adult communicants classes in the total adult program. The mistake is often made of limiting them in their scope to those coming into the church by confession or reaffirmation of faith, and those coming by letter of transfer from churches of other denominations. Yet the religious illiteracy of those transferring from other churches of the same denomination is often appalling. For various reasons a church may decide that it is best not to require their attendance at communicants class sessions; but at least they should be strongly urged to participate. I have found a high proportion of people in this category attending on a purely voluntary basis after they had been invited to attend. If the minister believes firmly in the special spiritual values of small groups, he will ordinarily schedule two or more identical sessions so that the number will be small enough to give his people a sample that will whet their appetites for further study in small groups. For many of them, this will be their first experience of this kind. Of course, the curriculum of a series of communicants class sessions cannot begin to give adequate coverage to the important doctrines of the church. Perhaps it is best if these classes serve to raise even more questions than they answer. This would help people to see that the " simple gospel " is not nearly so simple and pat as they had supposed, and might stimulate a desire to explore some of these questions more fully in continuing study groups. My own Sunday morning theological discussion group arose in this way, as members of each of the three identical communicants classes I had been conducting for six weeks requested further opportunity for study and discussion. If the minister has done a proper job of church officer training, many of his officers can share in the leadership of these classes, especially sessions on the church's polity, traditions, and practices.

FAMILY, NEIGHBORHOOD, AND JOB

The fact that most of the conscious needs and problems of our laymen center, as we have seen, around the home, the community, and the place of work suggests that we should organize our adult Christian education program so that, at least to some degree, it is functionally related to these main areas of concern. Within the dynamics of small interest groups following this pattern of immediate concern, it is possible to lead men and women toward the kind of encounter that may contain God's answer to their deepest needs.

Parent Education. The concern of the adult in regard to the quality of his family relationships provides an immediate point of contact for the church's adult education program. One should not be surprised if interest in a parents class turns out to be far greater than interest in the traditional adult Bible class, because of its functional concentration on an area of great concern to young and middle-aged couples. In many churches a direct approach to developing a strong program of general adult education may be only moderately successful in the breadth of its appeal and in the proportion of the adult congregation who become actively involved in it. A more indirect approach, starting with parents classes and moving out from there to more inclusive adult interests, may be much more successful in attaining a fairly high proportion of participation in the church's program of adult education.

The large parent-teacher type of meeting is useful for informing parents concerning the church school program and for insuring more intelligent, though rather general, co-operation. But although a church may need such mass meetings of parents and teachers for the general servicing of the teaching program in the church school, it chiefly needs to bring parents together in small groups for study so that they can better fulfill their own teaching ministry to their children. Of course, the parent-teacher meeting may serve admirably as an initial step in a program of parent education by confronting parents with their responsibility in a way that leads to personal conviction; for when parents are brought to acknowledge their responsibility, and take their first faltering steps toward meeting it, the way is opened for a fuller study program. When they undertake to discuss the content of the church school curriculum with their children, or to carry on any sort of coherent Christian conversation with them, they will discover how little they actually know, and they may find that many ideas they have long taken for granted must be re-examined. The church's program of parent education will then minister to conscious needs.

Starting from their natural and immediate concerns for their children, parents may be challenged to explore a rich variety of fields of study related to these concerns and also to the deeper concerns that underlie them. For example, when parents are stimulated to an awareness of the importance of the quality of family relationships for Christian education in the home, self-examination may lead to a desire for greater theological and psychological understanding of this area of personal relationships. In the same way, recognition of the influence of the mass-media and community conditions upon family life may lead to a study of relevant social issues.

Neighborhood Groups. The educational program of the typical church is concentrated for the most part in the church building. Except for the occasional parish visit and the literature that is mailed out, the members come to the church rather than having the church come to them. In practice, this tends to limit the proportion of the membership involved in the educational program of the church. A membership that is rather widely dispersed geographically is not easy to communicate with when the major means of communication are fixed at one spot in the city.

The church needs to " come out of its building," so to speak, and to come to life in homes in local neighborhoods, as it did in apostolic times before any churches had been built. Many churches have come to realize this, and have established what is variously known as the " zone plan " or the " colony system," whereby the parish is divided geographically into zone groups. However, the main purpose of such arrangements is usually only social and assimilative, or evangelistic, with the emphasis being on recruitment of new members, neighborhood get-togethers, and

systematic parish visitation. But such neighborhood groupings can also serve a more specifically educational function.
In many situations parent education can be carried on more
meaningfully along neighborhood lines than along age
group lines. A regional community of interest and friend-
ship might prove to be more cohesive and significant than
a community of interest based upon the coincidences of
children's ages. Of course, each zone or colony might pick
any particular field of religious interest for study, not
limiting itself to something that would only interest parents. Neighborhood groups have been used with great success as a natural form of organization for Lenten study
groups on topics of general adult interest, and in one church
several of these neighborhood groups have continued to
meet the year around.

Vocational Groups. Just as the minister as adult educator
should meet with the layman where he *lives,* so he should
meet with him where he *works.* The office or factory district may not lie in the parish zone plan, but nevertheless it
too can be a locus of significant adult Christian education
work. A great deal can be accomplished meeting with a
small group of laymen during the lunch hour. C. Wright
Mills has amply demonstrated the degree to which, in the
white-collar world, a man's personal identity is related to
his job. Alongside family and neighborhood identifications,
one's vocational identification is a field of great interest to
him. The depersonalization and bureaucratization of work
has resulted, paradoxically, in an alienation from work as
a source of meaning in life at the same time that social identification has become more closely related to one's position
in the American business hierarchy. Thus one's work is a
principal area of *concern,* and yet one in which little intrinsic *meaning* is seen — and surely little meaning in terms
of relevance between one's job and one's faith. Vocational

study groups, therefore, both start with a very important conscious interest and minister to a very great need. They provide opportunities for men to ask: " What purpose does my job serve in God's plan for his world? What are its limits? Are there certain aspects of my work that are inconsistent with the Biblical revelation? " The specific way in which these questions are posed and answered will, of course, vary greatly depending upon one's occupation. Therefore, vocational study groups can be most relevant when their members are all of the same general occupational category. The larger church is naturally in a better position to establish such specialized groups from within its own membership; yet the smaller church can carry on such activities in co-operation with other churches, or by concentrating on an occupational category that is well represented in its membership.

In vocational study groups, the laymen will furnish most of the data, most of the raw material for the discussion, since they are in the best position to understand their own particular temptations to irresponsibility and sharp practices and the ethical dilemmas of their occupation. The minister, as theological resource person in such groups, will not propose pat solutions to the complex ambiguities of vocational problems. He will only confront his laymen with the particular Christian themes that are relevant to their vocational predicament, trusting that in the dialogue between the two, new revelation may come to them — and to him.

EXPANDING THE PROGRAM

In considering the function of small study groups in the church, a word of warning must be spoken. It is important to recognize the demonic temptations to feelings of spiritual pride and exclusiveness which such groups often face.

The *ecclesiola in ecclesia*, the smaller Christian community within the larger Christian community, has, as we have noted, often been a powerful leavening influence toward spiritual rebirth and enlightenment for the entire congregation. Small groups, meeting for study and prayer, can revolutionize the life of a parish. But an almost inevitable by-product of such group experiences is the feeling that membership in the group more fully meets the demands of the Christian gospel. If such spiritual pride develops, it tends to sever the organic relation between the group and the church as a whole. The group then lives for itself or for its own ideals and disciplines instead of feeding leadership, ideas, and spiritual power into the ongoing life of the church that created it. The group derives its life from the life stream of the church and has a justification for its existence only as it contributes to that ongoing stream. The group should never exist for itself, but only to make membership in the total body of Christ more meaningful.

Very often the group may serve as " leaven in the lump " through the individual witness of its members and through the more informed and dedicated role they play in other aspects of the church's life. Sometimes the suggestion is made that such groups should adopt and plan service projects as a means of expanding their witness corporately. However, when this is done, the group can easily become so highly organized, and can spend so much time planning its project, that it ceases to be a study group in the truest sense. Of course, it is true that Christian education should bear fruit in Christian service; but there is no reason why this service must be in the form of a corporate undertaking by the group.

A service to the church, which is more appropriate to the very nature of a study group, is the expansion of the adult Christian education program of the church. As a vital

" cell " in the body of Christ, perhaps the best method of expansion would be the process of " cellular fission," the division of the existing group to form two or more new groups, which would involve others in the same sort of learning experience. The inclusion of new members in an existing group rapidly makes it unwieldy and unsuited for intimate personal interaction. But on the other hand, in many groups there may be considerable resistance on the part of the members to the suggestion that they break up to form the nuclei of leaders and participants for new groups. They may argue that an entirely new group should be started, without disturbing their new-found fellowship. Unquestionably, there are great spiritual values in belonging to an ongoing group that has been held together by a common urgency and purpose for a long period of time. But strong resistance to division usually indicates that the group has become ingrown upon itself, and that its members are placing their own personal satisfactions above the needs of other adults in the church. Something has gone wrong spiritually in the life of a group when it places a higher valuation on its own cohesiveness than on helping others to share in the same rich experiences its members have known together. Where there is such resistance to division, there is all the more reason for dividing the group. Obviously, the members should not be *forced* to do this. The minister must lead them to realize for themselves that the self-sacrificial death of their old fellowship can lead to new life for others, and that the group which seeks only its own life will surely lose it.

It is through the division of an original group or groups that the minister can best expand this type of program of adult Christian education without experiencing an unmanageable multiplication of demands upon his time and energy. Several of those in the original group or groups will have a backlog of experience, together with the necessary ability, to assume the leadership of new groups. The minister can, with a minimum of outside preparation, serve as informal resource person for these new groups, and eventually he may hand over even this responsibility to the group members. His role can evolve gradually from that of being leader of the original groups to that of holding seminars and personal conferences with his group leaders and visiting the groups occasionally as his schedule permits. In this way, the adult Christian education program can become, in time, a genuine *lay movement* in the church, with the minister functioning, in Richard Niebuhr's words, as " pastoral director " and " teacher of teachers."

Notes

Notes:

1. Earl F. Zeigler, *Christian Education of Adults* (The Westminster Press, 1958), p. 109.

2. Samuel W. Blizzard, "The Training of the Parish Minister," *Union Seminary Quarterly Review*, Vol. XI (Jan., 1956), No. 2, p. 47.

3. H. Richard Niebuhr raises this issue of unrelatedness and overspecialization in the curriculums of the seminaries in his book *The Purpose of the Church and Its Ministry*. In *The Teaching Ministry of the Church*, James D. Smart calls attention to the unfortunate dichotomy between the more traditional theological disciplines and the departments of religious education in the seminaries.

4. Unless otherwise indicated, statements concerning Dr. Blizzard's study are based on lecture notes taken in his course at Union Seminary entitled "Religion and the Social Sciences." Most of his findings have not as yet been published.

5. H. Richard Niebuhr, *The Purpose of the Church and Its Ministry* (Harper & Brothers, 1956), pp. 53–55. Quotations from this book are used by permission of the publisher.

6. Blizzard, "The Training of the Parish Minister," *loc. cit.*, p. 48.

7. Wayne E. Oates, *Anxiety in Christian Experience* (The Westminster Press, 1955), p. 151.

8. *Ibid.*, p. 152.

9. H. Shelton Smith, *Faith and Nurture* (Charles Scribner's Sons, 1950), p. 104.

10. Wesner Fallaw, *The Modern Parent and the Teaching Church* (The Macmillan Company, 1946), pp. 205, 210.

11. Lewis J. Sherrill, *The Gift of Power* (The Macmillan Company, 1955), p. 178.

12. Niebuhr, *op cit.*, pp. 63–67.

13. Calvin, *Tracts,* Vol. III, as quoted in Ainslie, *The Doctrines of Ministerial Order in the Reformed Churches of the Sixteenth and Seventeenth Centuries* (T. & T. Clark, Edinburgh, 1940), p. 208.

14. Daniel T. Jenkins, *The Nature of Catholicity* (Faber & Faber, Ltd., London, 1942), p. 101.

15. Luther, *Church Postil,* Vol. I, as quoted in *The Way of Discipleship* (Presbyterian Board of Christian Education, 1957), p. 63.

16. Ainslie, *op. cit.*, p. 40.

17. *Ibid.*, p. 66.

18. "The duties of ministers are various, which, however, most people restrict to two, *in which all the others are comprised,* the *teaching* of the gospel of Christ and the due administration of the sacraments." From the Second Helvetic Confession, as quoted in Ainslie, *op. cit.*, p. 44. Italics mine.

19. "Wherein the more or less sincerely, according to Christ's institution, the Word of God is *taught,* . . . the more or less pure are such churches to be counted." From the Irish Articles of Religion of 1615, as quoted in Schaff, *The Creeds of Christendom,* p. 538. Italics mine.

20. Wilhelm Pauck, "The Ministry in the Time of the Continental Reformation," *The Ministry in Historical Perspectives* (Harper & Brothers, 1956), edited by H. Richard Niebuhr and Daniel D. Williams, p. 135.

21. As quoted in Pauck, *op. cit.*, p. 137.

22. Richard Baxter, *The Reformed Pastor* (Sawyer, Ingersoll & Co., 1852), p. 68.

23. *Ibid.*, pp. 68–69.

24. *Ibid.*, p. 78.

25. *Ibid.*, pp. 71–72.

26. The *Scottish Book of Discipline* of 1560, as quoted in John Knox, *The Works of John Knox* (James Thin, Edinburgh, 1895), edited by David Laing, Vol. II, p. 241.

27. James D. Smart, *The Teaching Ministry of the Church* (The Westminster Press, 1954), p. 48.

28. Baxter, *op. cit.*, p. 34.

30. John T. McNeill, *The History of the Cure of Souls* (Harper & Brothers, 1951), p. 258.

31. Pauck, "The Ministry in the Time of the Continental Reformation," *loc. cit.*, p. 139.

32. F. W. Dillistone, *The Structure of the Divine Society* (The Westminster Press, 1951), p. 128.

33. Baxter, *op. cit.*, p. 24.

34. Gerald J. Jud, "Ministry in Colonies and Retreats," *Spiritual Renewal Through Personal Groups* (Association Press, 1958), edited by John L. Casteel, p. 80. Quotations from this book are used by permission of the publisher.

35. Howard B. Haines, "Fellowship Groups: Intercessory Love," *Spiritual Renewal Through Personal Groups* (Association Press), pp. 132–133.

36. Lewis J. Sherrill, *The Gift of Power*, p. 52.

37. Robert W. Lynn, "Experiment in Suburbia," *Spiritual Renewal Through Personal Groups* (Association Press, 1958), edited by John L. Casteel, p. 164.

38. Niebuhr, *op. cit.*, p. 82.

39. *Ibid.*, pp. 82–83.

40. *Ibid.*, p. 83.

41. Hendrik Kraemer, *The Communication of the*

Christian Faith (The Westminster Press, 1956), p. 27.

42. David Riesman, Nathaniel Glazer, and Reuel Denney, *The Lonely Crowd* (Doubleday & Co., Inc., 1953), p. 64.

43. William H. Whyte, *The Organization Man* (Simon and Schuster, Inc., 1956), p. 179.

44. C. Wright Mills, *White Collar* (Oxford University Press, 1951), pp. 161–188.

45. Riesman, *op. cit.*, p. 178.

46. *Ibid.*, p. 165.

47. Lewis J. Sherrill, *The Gift of Power*, p. 30.

48. Robert W. Spike, *In But Not of the World* (Association Press, 1957), p. 61.

49. Riesman, *op. cit.*, p. 219.

50. Charles D. Kean, *The Christian Gospel and the Parish Church* (The Seabury Press, Inc., 1953), p. 37.

51. Robert W. Lynn, "Experiment in Suburbia," *Christianity and Society*, Vol. XVIII (Spring, 1953), p. 21.

52. Everett C. Parker, David W. Barrie, and Dallas W. Smythe, *The Television-Radio Audience and Religion* (Harper & Brothers, 1955), p. 403.

53. *Ibid.*, p. 402.

54. Riesman, *op. cit.*, pp. 69–70.

55. Baker Brownell, *The Human Community* (Harper & Brothers, 1950), p. 127.

56. Theodore O. Wedel, *The Christianity of Main Street* (The Macmillan Company, 1952), pp. 2–5.

57. Will Herberg, *Protestant-Catholic-Jew* (Doubleday & Co., Inc., 1955), pp. 63 ff.

58. Kraemer, *op. cit.*, pp. 93–95.

59. Thomas M. Steen, "Renewal in the Church," *Spiritual Renewal Through Personal Groups* (Association Press, 1958), edited by John L. Casteel, pp. 34–35.

60. Earl F. Zeigler, *Toward Understanding Adults* (The Westminster Press, 1934), p. 54.

61. Randolph C. Miller, *Biblical Theology and Christian Education* (Charles Scribner's Sons, 1956), p. 191.

62. H. Richard Niebuhr, *op. cit.*, p. 92.

63. Everett C. Parker, David W. Barrie, and Dallas W. Smythe, *op. cit.*, p. 235.

64. Lewis J. Sherrill, *The Struggle of the Soul* (The Macmillan Company, 1955), pp. 113 ff.

65. Carl B. Jung, *Modern Man in Search of a Soul* (Harcourt, Brace and Company, Inc., 1939), translated by W. S. Dell and Cary F. Baynes, p. 264.

66. Robert W. Lynn, "Experiment in Suburbia," in *Spiritual Renewal Through Personal Groups*, p. 150.

67. Gerald J. Jud, "Ministry in Colonies and Retreats," *loc. cit.*, p. 84.

68. Arthur T. Jersild, *When Teachers Face Themselves* (Columbia University Press, 1955), p. 75.

69. Wayne E. Oates, *op. cit.*, pp. 152–153.

70. Paul Tillich, *The Courage to Be* (Yale University Press, 1953), p. 119.

71. Niebuhr, *op. cit.*, p. 94.

72. Paul Tillich, *Systematic Theology* (University of Chicago Press, 1953), Vol. I, p. 49.

73. Harold R. Fray, Jr., "The Spirit Making New," *Spiritual Renewal Through Personal Groups* (Association Press, 1958), edited by John L. Casteel, p. 78.

74. Lewis J. Sherrill, *The Gift of Power*, p. 82.

75. George F. MacLeod, *We Shall Rebuild* (Iona Community, Glasgow, 1947), p. 66.

76. Fray, "The Spirit Making New," *loc. cit.*, pp. 69–70.

77. Lewis J. Sherrill, *The Gift of Power*, pp. 88–90.

78. J. Gordon Chamberlain, *Revelation and Education*, an unpublished Ed.D. thesis, Teachers College, 1951, pp. 99–100.

79. Charles K. Ferguson, "Using Informal Methods," *Adult Leadership*, Vol. III (March, 1953), p. 24.

80. Harry A. and Bonaro W. Overstreet, *Leaders for Adult Education*, as quoted in Franklyn S. Haiman, *Group Leadership and Democratic Action* (Houghton Mifflin Company, 1951), p. 71.

81. Niebuhr, *op. cit.*, pp. 117–118.

82. J. Robert Nelson, *The Realm of Redemption* (The Epworth Press, London, 1951), p. 56.

83. *Ibid.*, pp. 54–56.

84. Daniel T. Jenkins, *The Gift of Ministry* (Faber & Faber, Ltd., London, 1947), p. 130.

85. Paul Bergevin and John McKinley, *Design for Adult Education in the Church* (The Seabury Press, Inc., 1958), p. 101.

86. Nelson, *op. cit.*, p. 57.

87. Kraemer, *op. cit.*, pp. 28–29.

88. Reuel Howe, *Man's Need and God's Action* (The Seabury Press, Inc., 1953), pp. 75–80.

89. Jud, "Ministry in Colonies and Retreats," *loc. cit.*, p. 98.

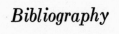

Bibliography

Bibliography:

DOCTRINE AND PRACTICE

Baxter, Richard, *The Reformed Pastor*. Sawyer, Ingersoll & Co., 1852.

Casteel, John L. (ed.), *Spiritual Renewal Through Personal Groups*. Association Press, 1958.

Jenkins, Daniel T., *The Gift of Ministry*. Faber & Faber, Ltd., London, 1947.

————, *The Nature of Catholicity*. Faber & Faber, Ltd., London, 1942.

Kean, Charles D., *The Christian Gospel and the Parish Church*. The Seabury Press, Inc., 1953.

Kraemer, Hendrik, *The Communication of the Christian Faith*. The Westminster Press, 1956.

Nelson, J. Robert, *The Realm of Redemption*. The Epworth Press, London, 1951.

Niebuhr, H. Richard, *The Purpose of the Church and Its Ministry*. Harper & Brothers, 1956.

Niebuhr, H. Richard, and Williams, Daniel D. (eds.), *The Ministry in Historical Perspectives*. Harper & Brothers, 1956.

GROUP DYNAMICS

Cantor, Nathaniel, *The Teaching-Learning Process*. The Dryden Press, Inc., 1955.

Clemmons, Robert S., *Dynamics of Christian Adult Edu-*

cation. Abingdon Press, 1958.

Haiman, Franklyn S., *Group Leadership and Democratic Action*. Houghton Mifflin Company, 1951.

Little, Sara, *Learning Together in the Christian Fellowship*. John Knox Press, 1956.

PHILOSOPHY OF CHRISTIAN EDUCATION

Howe, Reuel D., *Man's Need and God's Action*. The Seabury Press, Inc., 1953.

Sherrill, Lewis J., *The Gift of Power*. The Macmillan Company, 1955.

Smart, James D., *The Teaching Ministry of the Church*. The Westminster Press, 1954.

UNDERSTANDING THE LAYMAN

Psychology:

Jung, Carl B., *Modern Man in Search of a Soul*, tr. by W. S. Dell and Cary F. Baynes. Harcourt, Brace and Company, Inc., 1939.

Oates, Wayne E., *Anxiety in Christian Experience*. The Westminster Press, 1955.

Sherrill, Lewis J., *The Struggle of the Soul*. The Macmillan Company, 1955.

Tillich, Paul, *The Courage to Be*. Yale University Press, 1953.

Sociology:

Herberg, Will, *Protestant-Catholic-Jew*. Doubleday & Co., Inc., 1955.

Mills, C. Wright, *White Collar*. Oxford University Press, 1951.

Riesman, David, Grazer, Nathaniel, and Denney, Reuel, *The Lonely Crowd*. Doubleday & Co., Inc., 1953.

Whyte, William H., *The Organization Man*. Simon and Schuster, Inc., 1956.